Adv.
A Time to Mourn & A Time to Dance

"Phrase after visceral literary phrase, as if gasping for air, Jennifer Ohman-Rodriguez draws us into her home, where the horrific death of her husband is pummeling her and her two young sons. You'll be on the edge of your seat watching her navigate the emotional rubble of sudden trauma, face what death has ripped open, and recount the love story of her life. Jennifer shows how layering in trauma therapy help her discover a way to heal and embrace home again." **—Stan Tatkin, PsyD, MFT, co-founder of the PACT Institute, and author,** *We Do: Saying Yes to a Relationship of Depth, True Connection, and Enduring Love*

"Ohman-Rodriguez invites the reader into a circuitous journey of grief through staccato, punchy sentences. Her writing embodies how unexpected grief pummels a person like a relentless boxer, with gut punches one least expects. She opens a theological depth to grief which rejects sappy, happy endings but faces the depths of despair into which the Risen Christ accompanies. This is a book for those brave enough to enter and linger in grief embodied but who yearn for something more than platitudes to address the traumas of our time. If you have the courage to call wrenching grief what it is, you have a worthy companion in this book." **—Rev. Robin Steinke, President, Luther Seminary**

"*A Time to Mourn & A Time to Dance* is an honest, unconstrained, and unforgettable story of trauma, loss and healing. Ohman-Rodriguez weaves the deep elements of grief into the courage and strength she summoned to arrive at healing—'wind propelling us toward life, not away from it.' Her work is a profound and needed teaching about trauma recovery and perseverance, masterfully told." —**Paula D'Arcy, author, *Winter of the Heart and Stars at Night***

"The halting sentences that shape *A Time to Mourn & A Time to Dance* profoundly illustrate the physical, mental, and spiritual experience of halting grief. I experienced the author's writing style to model her own advice in the response to trauma, 'repeat small messages' and then as I read my own short and shallow breathing gave way to deep healing cleansing breath, not negating trauma and grief, but inhaling and exhaling hope. May her readers feel beckoned to breathe and pray through her witness of her own journey from mourning to dancing." —**Bishop Amy Current, Southeastern Iowa Synod, ELCA**

"With word pacing and pictures that grab your guts from the inside out, Jennifer Ohman-Rodriguez takes you on an intimate journey through death and survival. Readers witness depths of suffering while being guided into practices of healing centered in the pit at the foot of the cross." — **Rev. Jan Schnell, Ph.D., Assistant Professor of Liturgics, Wartburg Theological Seminary**

A Time to Mourn and a Time to Dance

A LOVE STORY OF GRIEF, TRAUMA, HEALING, AND FAITH

Jennifer Ohman-Rodriguez

chalice
press

Saint Louis, Missouri

ChalicePress.com

Print: 9780827237308
EPUB: 978082723731
EPDF: 9780827237322

A Time to Mourn and a Time to Dance

A LOVE STORY OF GRIEF, TRAUMA, HEALING, AND FAITH

Dedication

Family selfie in Santa Catalina State Park, Arizona.

In memory of Anthony Derayunan Rodriguez

Husband, partner, father, son, brother, friend, and healer of hidden wounds

And to our beloved sons, Paul and Ricardo,

my heart's blessings.

Contents

Prologue

What happened to us is unthinkable, unimaginable. My body reacts in life or death ways. For months, I grasp the sides of pain's deep pit, hanging on with my sons as my arms grow weary. The only way out? To heal. Allow others to lessen, eradicate, make well the ravages of trauma on our hearts, souls, bodies, and minds. Because healing is the only way to honor my late husband Tony, a licensed mental health therapist certified in trauma recovery.

Words printed on these pages: my story. A story told through the lens of our first sixteen months without Tony. Events as I experienced them—fragmented—choppy—not smooth prose. It's an inside look at how my brain could not function fully when shut down in the aftermath of trauma.

My sons have their own stories, not mine to tell. Yet they, my beloveds, weave in and out of this my story. I include them here with love and respect for their privacy, while I make public my intimate self. Bit by bit unfolding my captivity to grief and trauma's grasp, welcoming others in. Into hell's chaos. Into shards of hope. Into healing's slow balm.

Interspersed throughout my story are prayers and healing practices. Some I relied on to survive. Some I created for others from a more healed state. Use them—for yourself, for others. In including these prayers and practices, I pray my own version of the words of the psalmist: Let my words here be acceptable to God, the universe, Tony, our sons, and all who read our story.[1]

---

[1] Based on Psalm 19:14 (NRSV), "Let the words of my mouth and the meditation of my heart be acceptable to you O, LORD…"

I. Standing Statue

"For anyone with a heart, goodbye is hard. For anyone with a
heart, no goodbye shreds the soul to pieces."
—Jennifer Ohman-Rodriguez

First Evening

Light falls. Wind settles. Stars pop. Crickets toll around buildings
standing silent, stunned into shared tragedy.

Once back on the rented vacation farm, we separate into different spaces inside and out. Rescue team driving us back, using
our car. Someone loading the kayak in the parking lot back at the
beach. Maybe our sons. Tony's body gone in local coroner's van.
Heading somewhere. Away from us. Hear Tony's voice. One of his
many therapist sayings. What just happened here?

Paul, our fourteen year-old son, crawls into his sleeping
bag in the corner of the living room floor. Cocooning in safety. Perhaps still chilled by the day. Head phones silencing an
already quiet house. Curling up. Entering fatherlessness. Again I
hear Tony's commentary: The guy at ground zero goes into the
bunker.

Ricky, just a month into nineteen, wears weighty quiet.
Pacing the farm pasture across a long gravel drive leading to the
road. Moving, caged animal style. Stopping. Staring into the vast
darkening sky. Questioning. Raging. Body alive with betrayal.
Brain stem still fleeing the river's swallowing grasp.

I stand on deck, bile rising in throat. Aware of my children yet
incapable of mothering. Emotions frozen in my heart. Unable to

make decisions. No longer the person who hours ago loaded up the car for an afternoon of fun at local river's beach remembering towels, sun screen, nut allergy emergency kit, and a book to page through lazily.

Stand, lost. As if I'd left myself at the beach. Bringing home only my outer layer of skin. A shell. Standing statue. Thoughts moving in heavy dance. Future fuzzy. Praying for clarity. Slow motion determining my current responsibilities: What to do about them?

"What about the woman at ground zero?" Tony asks.

I wander back into the house. Check on Paul. Need to hold him. Try wrapping my shaking arms around him, but am barred from doing so. Ask inane questions in anxious interference instead. "How are you?" My words meet silence.

Ricky returns from the field's sanctuary. "We can't stay here tonight, Mom. We need to go home."

I listen because he may be right or because I need him to be right. Sounds so clear and convincing. But making decisions, making something happen, as I have so many times in the last two decades, seems a mountain too steep to climb. Decisions stall on top of thoughts. Freeze like my body back at the beach. Suspend like time. Drive? Home? Thought surfaces out of fog. "Neither you nor I can drive tonight."

Yet something pushes me toward home. My body wanting to run from the swirl of people surrounding us all day. To run from this painful place. Run toward our refuge. But how will we get home? Another obstacle to surmount.

"I'm calling Linnea and Tom," my mother says as if a phone call to our dear friends might keep us all from slipping into the abyss.

I nod, knowing they will come. Get us. Take us home.

My brother Peter settles his two daughters in the upstairs room of our rented place. Their young, restless bodies find sleep. But only after hours of wiggling. Then Peter drives to the end of the farm's long gravel drive. Smelling of an August meadow in goldenrod, cone flower, yarrow, milkweed. Parks. Waits under stars. Keeping vigil with his heart. His beaming headlights the only lighted signal for the help driving toward us.

Girls sleeping. Peter waiting. Paul cocooning. Ricky pacing again. My mother packing our things. Tony's things. Toothbrush, clothes, book. Stuff of his no-longer-life. Me, returning to deck. Remembering Tony saying just this morning, "I'd love to buy this place!"

Close eyes. Open again to truth. Feel lower arms ache. Aware fingers shake. Missing numbers on dial pad. Fighting crazy reception. No emergency number on church's answering machine. Call other pastor friends. Hear voice messages. Need a funeral home. Cannot think of one. Stomach clenches, clenches, clenches. Want relief. Want a pastor. Inaccessibility exploding with insurmountable pain. Torn apart soul rising into unforgiveness. How will I do this...whatever this is? How?

Palm buzzes. Text reads "Jennifer: Writing to you with a broken heart. Just received the news...Weeping for what this means for you and the boys."

Friend. Pastor, once ours, reaching out. Also named Peter. Cling to words. Grasping phone. Everything else slippery. Traction evaporating into distant stars. How does Pastor Peter know? Tony's family doesn't know he's gone yet. Only our nephew Joe. Paul texting Joe from the beach. Reaching out in shock and pain. Joe calling back. Right now readying for the most mature act of his twenty-something-year-old life. Taking deep breaths before telling his mother of the death of her only and beloved brother. She in turn, while carrying the weight of her own grief, telling her parents. Sparing me one unbearable job.

Pastor Peter's words typed hundreds of miles away give me breath. Much-needed hit of oxygen. Do I text back? Call? Does he? Time suspends surrounded by stars. Cloaked in night. Hear Pastor Peter's voice. Gentle tone bringing calm. Perhaps hope.

What do I say? Tony needs transportation home. That's what the coroner told me at the beach. It's the one task I'm supposed to do. Right now. Get him home. But not really home. Never to our home again. Never alive or in my arms or puttering around the kitchen or joking with the boys. Just home as in the area we live in. Until we enact the ancient ritual of laying to rest our dearly departed loved one.

Through other friends, Pastor Peter finds a local funeral home in Iowa City, Iowa. Not a place here. Not in middle-of-nowhere Wisconsin, where we sit as strangers. Unclear as to Tony's exact whereabouts right now. Coroner whisking him away with great efficiency. To a holding place. One unimaginable to me.

Soon male voice of funeral director takes over. Keeping me grounded until our friends arrive. After ten. Hugging us. Sharing tears. Silences. Heads shaking in disbelief. My brother Peter's voice, known since birth, taking charge. Loading up our bags. Hugging me as we leave. Onto roads paved in somber despair. Tom driving us. Linnea following. Caravan winding south on country roads and highways. Quiet echoing with hours of previous keening. Men's voices joining in sorrow. Plaintive, quiet timbres resonating into air. For us. For them. For one of their own gone too soon. All is not well. Nor will it be well. But right now, men's voices carry me forward into my recently rendered, torn-apart unknown.

Way Home

Ride in unlit night. Quiet as it is dark. Staring out window into what's left of our future. Now and then involuntary sighs escaping through slightly opened mouths. Lips still cracked from day's sun and accumulated dehydration. Small distress signals giving voice despite our collective numbness. Car's safety creating space to do so.

Just north of Mount Vernon, Iowa, we turn off the four-lane highway. Head south toward Solon. Two-lane roads dotted by occasional farmyard light. Home thirty minutes away or so. Through silence hear Tony's voice, as if he is with us, or telephoning in.

"The boys need to be debriefed," he tells me.

In identity, I'm still a good psychotherapist's wife. Only eight hours or so a widow. I know about intervention protocols and techniques from listening to Tony for years. Especially the two years he worked for an employee assistance program in suburban Milwaukee. Tony provided debriefings after workplace traumatic events: post office shootings, murder in a company's parking lot, train accident. After traumatic events, people need something. As soon as possible. Within forty-eight hours. I don't know what exactly. Or whether this term—debriefing—is still used. But I know there is something out there in trauma therapeutic interventions minimizing our possible long-term traumatic responses. Because trauma left untended or ignored develops into bigger problems such as PTSD.

Combing through trauma recovery books months later, I learn something. Trauma first aid at the beach had been necessary but was not given. Simple techniques minimizing the accumulation of stuck life or death energy in our bodies. As manageable as asking us to count ten trees along the shore line. Or feel the bottoms of our feet on the dirt. Or even asking us to look into their faces instead of away. Another wrong layered on this day. From driving into a packed parking lot at the beach. To being driven home now. Wrong. Not right. Just wrong.

Cling this night to Tony's voice. To his knowing voice. His voice I love. His voice I cannot live without. Know in my gut our sons need something. Focus on them. Forget about me. Do not realize I am in post-traumatic shock, needing intervention as well. Tony's voice fades, leaving me again wondering what I heard. Thinking God forgive me. I don't know what I am doing. Not capable of planning ahead.

Two in the morning. Almost home. Ten minutes away. Driving on Mehaffey Bridge Road. Along the lake. A large, antlered deer leaps out onto our path. Tom swerves. Grazing the deer. It runs into the woods. We sigh in collective chorus. Each thinking, what awful thing next?

Home. Crawl into bed. Alone. Insides spinning. Saying over and over and over again "I forgive myself. I forgive myself. I forgive myself."

Anything to ward off the last moments of Tony already haunting me.

Sleep fitful. Tears sliding. Pillow wet.

Sunday

House throughout night full of small noises. Pain and shock audible through closed doors. I doze toward morning. Sun beginning predictable ascent into the sky. Phone rings early. Around seven. Waking our collective broken sleep. "Got your message. What's going on?" Pastor Ron asks.

What message? Vague, fuzzy memory pokes me. He doesn't know. Can't respond. How do I tell him? Have no words. "Tony." Silence. "Tony. Died. Yesterday."

"What?"

Body retracts into stomach, swallowed within, denying his disbelief. I hang up. Enter closet. Strip off all of yesterday. Stand naked, cold. Touch dress on hanger. Slip fabric into hands. Slide arms in and overhead. Cloth falling down. Covering what is left. In black. A shell.

House heavy in quiet. Linnea makes tea. We sit on green couch downstairs. Talking. Not talking. Sipping tea. Silent tears sliding down our cheeks into cups. Sons staying in their rooms. Sleeping or escaping or both. Think Ricky's dearest friend stayed the night. Talking into wee hours of morning out on trampoline. Found them there in my wanderings, unable to sleep. Calmed by Ricky's voice. Soothed by Paul's rhythmic breath.

Linnea makes plans for others to stay with us. Reinforcements for when they leave. She's conscious I can't be alone. Just the three of us. Constituting a family. She having witnessed through the last decade the countless hours we spent without Tony. He traveling. Building career and business. Working long hours away from us. Understanding we operated together or apart as a family of four. Until yesterday.

Midmorning, therapist friend Patrick shows up. He knows something about abruptly becoming fatherless too soon in life. Patrick spends time with Ricky and Paul. Gives a sort of therapeutic debriefing. Combined with a walk with Ricky. "A walk and talk," as Tony called it. Sits on the front stoop with Paul, then me. Before going with Ricky to Tony's clinical practice, The Men's Center, to help Ricky send out notifying email to clients, or perhaps he just bears witness to what Ricky must do. As a son. As a son doing administrative work for his therapist father. Now in the worst circumstances possible.

People travel toward us. Mom and cousin Naomi on their way. Naomi driving. No one thinking my mother should drive under the circumstances. Tony's sister, our nephew, and some of our nieces packing their bags. Peter's wife boarding an airplane on another continent. Our home's quiet is about to unravel. Cacophony approaching. Know our people must come. Fear what little control I have left will vanish in the noise.

Afternoon. People congregate in living room. Mom, cousin Naomi, Pastor Ron, Ricky, Paul, me. Recently arrived people working at internal calmness but radiating discomfort instead, colliding with my frozen anguish. Pastor Ron's voice too grating. Naomi's laugh too loud. Mom's chatter too much. I close my eyes, pray for silence without praying. Hold in my heart the person I most need for survival—another sudden widow. Someone with already acquired first-hand knowledge of this unstoppable pain permeating every fiber of my existence. A first-line savior traveling toward us. En route from Minnesota. My aunt, Linda.

Obituary

There are things I must do now. "I'll need an obituary," the funeral director tells me. Sit on our bed. In another black dress. Laptop open. Arms shaking. Words forming slowly. Capturing Tony's presence on this earth. Mind spinning with cruel chant. I can't do this. I can't do this. I can't do this. Then I write,

Anthony D. "Tony" Rodriguez, 53

Anthony Derayunan Rodriguez died suddenly and unexpectedly on Saturday, August 13, 2016. Those who knew and loved him called him "Tony." He called everyone "friend."
Tony was born on May 7, 1963, in Manila, Philippines, to Rick and Hope Rodriguez. The family immigrated to the United States in December of 1968 for Rick's work as a civil engineer. They settled in Chicago to be near extended family.

A professor at the University of Wisconsin at Milwaukee where Tony earned his bachelor degree recognized his innate abilities to serve others through the art and craft of mental health therapy. With this support, Tony went on to graduate from Loyola University Chicago with a Master of Social Work degree. He then became a Licensed Clinical Social Worker, which was his calling and passion.
Tony met his wife, Jennifer Ohman, on October 1, 1994. They married on August 5, 1995. Tony and Jennifer welcomed two beloved sons into their union. Ricardo Rodriguez and Paul Rodriguez. Tony and Jennifer were married twenty-one years.

In 2003, Tony felt called to serve as a therapist to adult men surviving childhood sexual abuse and violence. He opened his business, The Men's Center, with the tagline "A place for healing, mindfulness, and possibilities" the following fall. During this time Tony served as a board member for the international group, Male Survivor. He expanded his work a few years later to serve people living with and suffering from sexual addictions and compulsions. In 2011, Tony and two colleagues wanted to fill a gap in the therapeutic literature realizing the need for a resource for partners of people suffering from sexual addictions. They wrote and published *Facing Heartbreak: Steps to Recovery for Partners of Sex Addicts*. This book is widely used throughout the world. Tony presented workshops, too many to name, for other therapists throughout the United States. Tony's work, the work he felt called and compelled to do, impacted many lives.

Tony leaves a great hole in his passing. He was a man of great faith in a loving and grace-giving God, as well as in the ability of people to heal, and the primacy of relationships in our lives. He loved with a whole heart, worked to eradicate the shame surrounding sexual violence and sexual addictions, and lived each day with integrity, a warm smile, and the willingness to keep loving and building his relationships and to help others to do the same.

Monday

Sit at table's head. In another black dress. Gaunt from shock, lack of sleep, poor intake of nutrients. Legs wound tightly around each other. Once. Twice. Arms armoring me. Upright. Still. Oxygen stealing through skin. Avoiding lungs.

I am the only known person bearing witness to Tony's last moment alive. Trying-to-make-sense-of-what-happened. I am still at the beach. Not here in a meeting room full of people. Sons, me, Pastor Ron, Aunt Linda, mom, Peter, funeral director. At a long conference table. Sitting in coolness. Outside cloaked in August heat. Planning the unplannable. Bumpy dynamics ricocheting off wallpapered walls. Noting too many people present. Too many opinions guised in helping postures. Forcing tiptoes in widowed diplomacy. Resentment rising. Mine.

Blog Comment

Phone buzzes with texts. Social media traffic soars. Email inbox fills. Thoughts from friends, family, and death business communications. Resent it. Avoid it. Want to throw up on it all. One message persists. Stands out. Response to a blog post I posted weeks ago. Message written two days after Tony's death. Words from woman praying. With husband on beach. Waiting for first responders. Stranger with toddler looking at us kneeling in the sand. Strangers surrounding my pain. Shielding me from all else.

> "Hi Jennifer,
>
> I'm the stranger who prayed with you Saturday afternoon. I looked you up and found your beautiful blog as well as learning about Tony's impact on so many people on his website. You and your boys are in my prayers every day, along with my family and the other family who was with us that day. Your comments in this article about what Lillian's stitches teach you – to keep breathing stitch by stitch – brought tears to my eyes. Keep breathing..."

Undone

Hear small snippet of sung liturgy. Over and over in my head. "Spirit intercedes for us with sighs too deep for words to express."[2] Based on a text from the apostle Paul's letter to the Romans.

"Likewise the Spirit helps us in our coming un-done-ness; for we do not know how to pray as we ought, but that very Spirit intercedes with groanings too deep for words. And God, who searches the heart, knows what is the mind of the Spirit."[3]

Am undone. No longer know how to pray. Only sigh, sob, hear these words praying for us.

Tuesday. Maybe Wednesday

Morning. Ease out of our bed. Another night of sort-of-sleeping. Falling asleep last night with nerve endings pinging through-

---

[2] "The Spirit Intercedes for Us" in *Evangelical Lutheran Worship* (Minneapolis, MN: Augsburg Fortress, 2006) #180.

[3] Romans 8:26–27 (NRSV) combined with Dr. David Frederickson's class translation and translation from Accordance Bible Software.

out body. Ping. Ping. Ping. Like shards of glass hitting skin from inside. Erupting in small tremors. Creating rolling, roaring waves in stomach. Contents crashing into esophagus. Sleep three, four hours. Toss for two, stemming off repetitive instant replay. Scene at river. Veins coursing with breath's life but with something else as well. Throbbing feeling of agitation filling arms, circulating throughout body. Waking me again and again. Crying out to the night, "Is this what combat vets feel?"

Sleep follows tossing in fit-filled few hours. Two, three, rarely four. Until early light demands my presence. Outside, on deck. Watching the world in incomprehension. While others sleep.

Last night, Ricky crawled into bed with me. His warmth filling up Tony's side. Saying, "I'm sorry you lost the love of your life."

Scampering then out of the house. Staying up and away until I rise as he sleeps. This morning finding Aunt Linda sitting at kitchen table sipping coffee. "I'm firing Pastor Ron," I announce.

My second firing in less than three days. The first, a heavyset man looming before me in Bermuda shorts. Telling me in a grated, nasal voice, "There's really no hope."

At beach I froze. Gluing myself to earth. Thin hospital blanket covering me in August heat. Water bottle nearby perhaps opened. Not drunk from. Thirsty as we waited. Yearning for water to saturate basic need. Yet wet from being in the water. Shivering. Damp as minutes pass into hours. World spinning every time I stand up. Three moments on beach causing me to react. Calling for help as Tony slipped away, my first reaction. Second, finding the rescue team's point person. "Who's this guy?" I ask. "The one in the shorts?"

"He just retired. He did my job."

"Get rid of him or I will implode!" I say.

Man goes quickly. No goodbyes. No apologies. Leaving only truth. Mine to ask for, not his to tell. Third time my body reacts by moving away. Separating myself from an awful woman in a large kayaking group. Curious about all the siren vehicles filling the packed parking lot. The yellow tape sectioning off ground zero. "What's going on?" she asks.

Turn my back. Walk away. Me, the suffering one this beautiful summer day.

Three days later, fourth firing. Of my pastor, Ron. Aunt Linda slowly sipping her coffee. "Good," she says.

There are other firings as days pass into weeks, months. Ricky, briefly. He thinking Tony left him in charge. That firing freeing him from his self-imposed expectation to stay home now as eldest child. Fire a few friends showing only horror at what happened. An educator. Finally, a high school, with the exception of a few teachers.

Join Aunt Linda with cup of tea. Leave it untouched. Sigh. Begin what I do not want to do. What must be done. Plan Tony's funeral. But really, Aunt Linda takes charge. Leaving me alone staring into air. Asks me questions only when necessary. Bearing complexities of our situation. "Who do you need to hear preach?" she asks.

Accessing needs difficult in swirling space of awfulness. Numb. Yet full of odd, stiff movements and thoughts. Answer hours later choking on words. "I need the same voice I heard. Over the phone. That first night. Coming out of nowhere. Standing on that strange deck. Far from home."

My brother steps in. Makes the call. Pastor Peter agrees. Issues arise and need to be dealt with. Complications I am not capable of handling. Forced to think despite my inabilities. Renovations continue on church building. Portable air conditioning unit pumps air into sanctuary. But it's August in Iowa. Heat high. Humidity unbearable. Want to be comfortable for the service, not sweating. Last time we worshiped in this space just what? A couple of weeks ago? Both Tony and Paul suffered asthma attacks caused by construction dust. Refuse to put Paul through this possibility on the day we bury his father. Ask to move the service to another church. Other large ELCA Lutheran congregation ruled out. Pews squeak. Refuse to listen to these sounds at Tony's funeral. I don't have to be easy to work with right now.

Roman Catholic congregation near us, one we occasionally worship with, turns us down for a Lutheran service in a Roman Catholic space. Lack of hospitality under the circumstances hurts. Blankets pain. Tell funeral director of Tony's healing work with male survivors of priest abuse. Tony received checks for his work with victims from this Catholic diocese, ranked high for sexual abuse cases. Now in death no room at the inn, leaving us struggling for one morning of shelter for this healer.

Another Roman Catholic congregation across town agrees. Surrounding people seem to think this choice nice for Tony's traditional Catholic family of origin. Maybe. Tony's family whirling in waves of shock. Not even knowing the whole story. Acting in a world made instantaneously unknown. Until months later when sons and I tell most of the story. Fragment by fragment. Tony's parents insist on having another service the morning after the funeral with the priest. We do not attend.

Told there is a Rodriguez family burial plot in Chicago. Don't remember knowing about it. Now refusing Tony's burial there. Too far away. Sons agree. Instead, three of us drive to local Iowa City cemetery. Meet person in charge and wish that Don, the funeral director, could be with us, as our agent in grief. Walk with this stranger through available plots. "You'll need a double," man tells me.

Undone already by choosing Tony's grave. Now must think of mine as well? Pick out a wooded plot in newer part of cemetery. Not crowded. "Dad will want shade," I remember saying to the boys. As if Tony cared now.

Sons agreeing with silence. Grave site bordering city park. Access to trail head nearby. One Tony and I hiked once on our lunch hour with Thunder, our chocolate labradoodle. Got very lost. Crabby. Worried about missing appointments. Still good thoughts warm my heart, memory being funny that way. The cemetery's adjoining park contains meaning. Right now, I'm needing all meaning available.

After day of planning, evening sinks into my darkness. Stand again at deck's rail. Gaze out over field, acres of corn or soybean, woods beyond. Night buzzing. Last chirps of birds before sleep. Humidity abating. Still swathed in black fabric. Cold in the heat. Railing keeping me upright. World before me, senseless. Thinking again, how will I do this? Not even sure what "this" is.

Poison Ivy.

"Where are the boys?"

Their absence quiets our home. Quiets all present. Except my internal workings. Apprehension mounting within.

"They went off into the woods," someone says.

How did I miss their leaving? Maybe trying to nap. Assuming others as hypervigilant in safety as this new version of me. But those who help us now live in bodies not mine. Mine knows their whereabouts when home. Sensing their chemicals, part mine. Smelling them as only a mother can. Knowing Paul stays close for the most part. Ricky out and about. Usually late at night, while the house pretends to sleep. Only giving in to my lack of control from midnight to dawn. Still knowing of his absence as I rest.

My body watches the woods. Slightly turned toward the window. Reminiscent of watching them in the water just a few days ago. Glancing. Glancing again. Eyes searching stretch of wooded creek land near our home. Waiting for their emergence. Again.

They haven't been in the woods together for years, I think. Maybe an utterance offered to the assembled. Watch again. Wait. Stand guard. Alarm growing in belly. Where are they?

"How long have they been gone?" I ask.

"Not long," someone tells me. Maybe Aunt Linda. Maybe my mother. Not showing concern.

Mine mounting. Into throat. Exploding through arms. Breath stuck in an intake. Waiting to exhale. Hours go by. Really minutes. Two figures emerge through trees. Walk across field. Two lanky, brown-haired boys. Taller one carrying a gun. "Why do they have a gun?"

No one answers me. Sons walk into garage entering house through mudroom. Smelling of earth, woods, August. "Where were you?" My voice pitches high.

"I took Paul out to show him how to shoot," Ricky answers.

Both are muddy. In shorts and short sleeves. Ricky holding a BB gun he bought. Something he's always wanted. Parents not supportive at all. Forgive them now. Ricky standing up as a man in some ancient way. Out hunting. Passing skills on. Making sure our table's always full. Taking over for absent father, the one who never held a gun in his life.

Hours later, maybe a day, Ricky and Paul complain of red, itchy rashes on their legs and arms. Crap! I think, poison ivy. Ask Aunt Linda to take me to Walgreens. Haze descending on each aisle. Freeze in front of anti-itch creams. In black dress surrounded by white floors, walls, lights. Sorrow glaring off sterility.

Can't think. Can't read. Aunt Linda offering suggestions. Buying every brand of poison ivy medication available. Hurrying them home. Demanding application immediately. Mind racing. You will not itch through your father's funeral!

Visitation

Tony's family arrives in waves in the days prior to visitation. They take Ricky and Paul shopping for suits. Put together photos for visitation. Clean up kitchen. Hold my hand.

But visitation day blurs. Put on black chiffon dress. Bought on sale rack a couple of weeks before Tony died. Pull hair back in ponytail. Humidity causing curls. Not able to deal with sudden unruliness. Arrive at funeral home early. See Tony for the first time since sitting in the ambulance at beach. Approach coffin, small, high-pitched sounds erupting from my chest.

Stand as extended family. Near coffin. Bottled water nearby. Long line snaking through corridor. See people known to me. Family, friends, church members, a few neighbors. Also see unknown people sitting near casket. Eyes tearing up. Heads shaking. Hands writing small goodbyes on slips of paper dropped like tears into a basket.

One by one Tony's clients grasp my arm. Pour out love for him, us. Hold me up with their respect. Gift us with healing journeys shared with Tony. Knowing him in a way our friends, neighbors, and even family did not and could not, through an intimacy of human exchange of hurt for healing balm. We hear over and over again, "He saved my life." Ricky, Paul, and I know those words are not figurative. Tony, our beloved, literally saved lives.

More testimony pours out of couples waiting in winding line. "Tony saved our marriage." Me knowing his true motivational focus: the marriage's children. Strengthening the coupleship translates into saving pain.

Over and over again, we hear these words. Emotions shared by strangers. Keeping me afloat in midst of public display of grief mixed with truth. Centering me on what Tony's life meant in our small section of the world. Words about why we as a couple made the decisions we did. Of the sacrificial nature of our life together. The foundation necessary for him to do his healing work. I cannot understand why Tony died. But I fully understand why he lived.

After visitation, Tony's sister Riphanie shares conversation she and Tony had just the previous May. "Tony told me if anything ever happened to him, we were to follow your wishes."

Relief floods me in visitation room. Still standing guard to our story, our love, Tony's casket. Claiming ownership of his remains as widow. As last one seeing his living beauty. The one sleeping in an empty bed. Waking each morning to widowhood's reality. Now doing death's work.

Funeral

Morning dawns bright. Promising heat. Seven days into pain. It is Friday, August 19, 2016. Tony's funeral today. At eleven.

Last four days people swirl around me. Planning. Asking questions. More questions. What scripture readings? Can't remember any. Bible suddenly foreign to me. Hearing one passage. In repetition. "If I speak in the tongues of mortals and of angels, but do not have love, I am a noisy gong or a clanging cymbal..."[4]

Words read at weddings dripping emotional syrup. Read at ours as well. Text meaningless without this gong part. Without pointing out needless words we all speak filling up space with nervousness or something. Noise grating away on our souls. That was never Tony's way. His words were few. Pointed. Usually powerful. No gonging. Choose this scripture text to be read for all to hear. It'll be the only spoken text for the day. Other scripture heard in song. Hymns about God's call to us. "God's ask" important to Tony and me. Add Nunc Dimittis. Simeon's song, some call it. Words of the old priest when he meets the boy Jesus: "Now dismiss your servant in peace. For my eyes have seen your salvation, which you have prepared in the sight of all nations."[5]

Tony lived as servant to humanity. I honor this about him. Lift it up. Call it out. It's all that he did not do in his own humbleness, and it's all I am willing to do this day when I cannot fully feel my fingers or emotions. Cry out what I know to be true even as my love for him feels buried under the emotional rubble left from the day he died.

People gear up. Bulletins appear. Pianist practices. Lutheran hymnals find places in Roman Catholic pews. Our congregation's

---

[4] 1 Corinthians 13 (NRSV).

[5] Luke 2: 29–31 (NIV).

baptismal shroud travels across town and is lovingly draped over Tony's casket. Sparkling in its beauty. Reminding us of something deeper than death: love.

Ricky types away at computer minutes before we must leave. Finalizing his eulogy. I tuck mine into my purse. Sigh. Check clock. Sigh again.

Aunt Linda will preside over holy communion. I assume the Catholic Church knows this, but really, I don't care. No energy for these differences. Other decisions made around me without my knowledge. Funeral director makes comments about moving mountains. Words wash over me. They are not important. Priest learns minutes before service of Aunt Linda presiding over holy communion. News filtering into our private room as we wait. Fidget with hair. Wring hands. Stand. Sit. Stand again in pain's pit. Imagine exchange, priest to funeral director. Words I will never know. Funeral director taking heat for me. Smile erupts. Trepidation freed by sorrow. Pushing limit despite pain. Same priest attends funeral. Sits in chair behind lectern. Looking grumbly. Me not understanding his presence. His affect not welcomed in my sorrow. Empathy for him not my responsibility this day.

When it's time to sing Simeon's words, the pianist misreads the bulletin, skips ahead to the recessional hymn. Nerves or grief impacting a moment. My empathy emerges. Feel her pain mix with mine. Watch wave of clerical robes rise across sanctuary. Cue Rachel to stop playing. No Nunc Dimittis today. Whisper words learned as a child. Now let your servant go in peace...

First Date

We met at work. Sixty-third and Kedzie. South side of Chicago. Tony, a licensed clinical social worker. I, a new hire into the agency's pilot Head Start program. Introduced first in staff meeting. Required in my new role to meet with each clinician individually. After several meetings in institutional looking offices, I enter Tony's space.

Darker than other offices. Lit with table lamps. No overhead fluorescents buzzing with background noise. Art adorning walls. Post cards plastering bulletin board over his desk. Desk up against the wall next to the door—not as barrier between people—making a statement of equality.

Learned our apartments separated by a few blocks, in the yet-to-be trendy old Swedish turned Middle Eastern and LGBTQIA+ neighborhood of Andersonville. His on Olive Street, mine on the corner of Glenwood and Berwyn.

Tony invited me to a party at his apartment the first Friday of my new job. I declined. This job in my mind constituted a temporary stop in life. No need to grow roots in its soil. Necessary for bill paying while circulating my résumé. We run into each other. At the copy machine. Tony wearing motorcycle boots, South American vests, and round tortoiseshell glasses. Looking focused and serious. Passing each other on the street to and from lunch. Stopping to chat. Me admiring his leather coat. Wondering silently and with interest what kind of man wears an olive-green leather coat. Reaching out to touch the lapel. Not realizing my wordless attraction. Sending a signal. An age-old, biological sign.

A few weeks later Tony invites me over for dinner. Thinking he's safe, maybe gay, I agree, not thinking it a date. Not dressing like it either. Ready to walk over from my apartment. Tony calling. Insisting on picking me up. In his black sports car. Heading for the grocery store.

Tells me years later it was all part of his plan. Doing something mundane like grocery shopping together. Testing our compatibility. Me thinking it a miracle I passed the test. Slightly frustrated at the store. Making him put items back on the shelf. Insisting on less expensive brands. Finding two-for-one deals on olive oil and spices. Getting hungry and a bit cranky.

Back at his apartment he cooked. I watched and talked. He seemed comfortable in his kitchen. No stranger to stove or oven. Sliding salmon and focaccia bread in. Checking the clock. Fussing a bit with marinade. Maybe tossing a salad. If there was dessert, I don't remember. Not serving wine or beer. Telling me he's not much of a drinker. Me thinking, that's different. Sitting down to dinner in his actual dining room. His apartment an old building built to house family. Now home to young, childless professionals. Talking (details long forgotten). Eating. Food delicious. Interrupted midway through dinner. Front door opening, echoing off hardwood floors. Roommate arriving home. Tony's emotions surfacing. Cloaked anger pouring out with good manners. Coolness directed toward roommate. Discovering in that moment the status of this dinner: a date.

Roommate leaves. We clean up. Again, I mostly watch from a kitchen stool against the wall. He takes off a flat silver chain link bracelet maybe half-an-inch in width. To wash the dishes. Men in my clan not bracelet wearers. Sexy, I think. Places bracelet on counter close to my perch. I put it on. The coolness of metal soothing my warm skin. In thickness of a man's bracelet. Not a woman's thin band. Run my finger over its chains. Something different here. I'm not sure I took the bracelet off until it broke years later.

We sat on the couch talking then. I snuggled up on my end, tired. My job emotionally draining. By Fridays feeling limp. Me often falling into bed early. Already eleven this night. Bolting up announcing I had to go home. Startling my host. Happy with how the evening was progressing.

Then I could not leave. More talking until very late. Tony drives me home. Nights never fully safe in our neighborhood. In the car Tony asks about former boyfriends. Not liking the little I tell him. Seems odd to me; after all, we are both thirty, and besides, he's had just as many former girlfriends as I have past boyfriends. Sense jealousy in this outwardly calm man.

We lunch next, I think. Food across the street from the agency in a Middle Eastern dive type of a place. Maybe we eat in my empty classroom. Maybe the restaurant. Maybe there is more than one lunch. Then it's my turn to invite him over for dinner. I buy a new outfit. Don't wear it. Plan a menu, French. Tarragon chicken with zucchini. Risotto. Poached pears in raspberry sauce. Wash the sheets. Straighten up the apartment. Over the phone, my sister-in-law teases me.

Tony arrives clad in a South American tunic. "Where are your door beads?" He wonders.

"What are you talking about?"

To him I seem like an earthy white girl. Long blond hair. Wrinkled clothes. No make up. His perception is I should have a sixties theme going on in my apartment.

And that's it. It wasn't the poached pears. Tony barely touched dinner. But within a week of this "dinner" date, I arrive home from work one evening. Trip over seven pairs of his shoes. Lined up neatly in my entry way. Discover my closet full of his sports jackets. Find a rice cooker in the kitchen. "What does this mean?" I ask a friend. "It's like he's moved in!"

"Jen, I think he's serious," she replies.

Eulogy

Shoe heels click across floor. Walk up a few steps. Arms wrap around Ricky. Thank him for his music and spoken tribute to his father. Then I place my words on the lectern and adjust the microphone. Look out at the assembly beginning to my left. Sweep through every pew, before speaking with slowness. Each consonant articulated, echoing off the walls, ceiling, and floors.

I have written and rewritten and rewritten my words for this day over and over and over again. Always in the deep of night when our home was as quiet as it can be in a time of raw grief. Always in my head, words spinning in and out of my heart. Never enough or the right words to encompass and capture my husband's life nor my love for him.

When I was thirty and fast approaching thirty-one, I was unemployed on purpose and nearing the point of running out of money. Dragging my feet, I accepted a position as a Head Start teacher in a large social service agency in Chicago where I worked on the south side at Sixty-third and Kedzie. At the same time, I was wondering why it was I could not seem to find or meet someone to share my life with and in a moment of budding faith I prayed to God to meet someone who treated me with the same respect my father did and always had.

One week later on the first day of my new job—the job I didn't really want—I met Tony.

A few months later my reserved Swedish, Minnesotan farm boy father literally leapt out of his chair in an act of uncharacteristic yet joyous emotion when Tony and I shared our wish to marry. My mother and I went into shock over my dad's behavior. But Tony laughed. And he laughed with that lovely, melodic laugh he had whenever he found delight in life. And thus, we went forward committed to each other and to the life we were building. Through times of immense joy such as the births of our two beloved sons, Ricky and Paul. And also through times of hardship such as the struggle to build our business, The Men's Center.

Tony reveled in fatherhood. Ricky and Paul: Dad loved you with a strength, passion, and depth that always astounded me. And he knew and told me, and anyone who listened, of his love and pride in both of you. You miss him so terribly now because Dad willingly and actively built love with you each and every day. As I watch you now through this very difficult week, I bear witness to you both using the emotional strength you built with and learned from Dad.

I want to say a few words about Tony's work, for it was his calling. In the spring of 2004, Tony returned late from a conference in Minneapolis. He sat on our bed in tears and told me what he needed to do, which was open The Men's Center. To do so meant leaving the security of corporate America. And it also meant long days and nights away from us, and many times an empty checkbook.

But I said "yes." Not because I wanted to but because I knew what Tony wanted to do was truth. So, I signed up for a tough journey, an often lonely one for me, but one I do not and have never for more than a few hours at a time regretted.

That was about twelve years ago. In that time Tony coached, healed, and taught many people. He used to say he didn't do kumbaya therapy. Instead he pushed people to do the hard stuff, "the heavy lifting" he called it, because he refused to gloss over the real issues at hand. He taught others but he also taught me and the boys. Tony taught me that home is where we do the hard, emotional stuff of life through uncomfortable conversations in which we face our past and present shame. He taught me to stay in the space even when I wanted to avoid an issue. And the list goes on and on. Last April I woke up one morning, sat up in bed telling my husband it was time for me to go to seminary. Tony's response was "finally."

So, we came full circle from my saying yes to his call to his saying yes to mine. What a gift. What an incredible gift. One I will cherish along with all the gifts of our life together for the rest of my life.

I close with a few words about the afternoon of Saturday, August 13. That day was an awful, traumatizing day. It was a day no one wants to experience or endure. But we did.

On that day we were surrounded by so much love, care, professionalism, and prayer. Our first responder team treated all of us with dignity always mindful of our needs as we waited, hoped, and then grappled with our new reality. And their care of Tony was so very tender and loving.

Mom and Peter, you were there with us that day, in shock and grieving too. Yet you both did the work of family, helping us in any way you could. Linnea and Tom, you sprang into action, dropping your lives, to assist in our journey home and reentry into our forever changed lives. Pastor Peter you reached out immediately, your voice over the phone that night keeping me grounded when I just wanted to drift away. Patrick, you listened. Nephew Joe, you did some heavy lifting. And Aunt Linda, you packed your bag and made ready to begin your work this week as our shepherd. So, I can only think and believe that, even as Tony left us that day, he arranged for us to be cared for and loved using the hands and hearts of others. And that care and love from others, some of whom were complete strangers to us and us to them, Tony would say is "gospel."

And I agree.

Walks

I stand in new expensive black dress, one that Mom bought me few days ago. Dress found after eating at Middle Eastern restaurant in a campus town the previous Monday after a grueling meeting with funeral director. Too many people at the planning table. Afterwards eating because I was hungry, novelty already. Craving something spicy. My brother and I stealing a few quiet moments away. From children. From others. From grief.

Finish eating. Wait outside on a sunny bench. Warm, late-August sun holding me. Forcing tired eyes closed. Escaping. Allowing time to stop. Peter maybe using bathroom or chatting with a stranger or paying the bill. Inner fog clouding ability to know or care. Only understanding no one expects me to pay for a meal now.

Eyes flick open. See a dress shop across street, a shop once housed beneath Tony's office about a half mile away. Replaced by another fast-food restaurant over on Washington Street. Rise. Cross street. Paw through sidewalk sale rack. Remember Tony encouraged me to shop here. Did once. Whiffed at the prices. Not my price range.

Three black dresses later, I walk around inside the store wearing one. Across the street, Peter stands on the sidewalk. Looking up the street. Then down. Scanning area for a glimpse of me. I walk outside. Waving. "Over here!"

Sweaty, puffing, yet gracious and funny, he walks in. "I thought you'd walked home," he said.

"It's a long way," I reply. Walk home from here an eight-mile hike. In a black dress, possibly heels. In Iowa's August humidity, heat. Peter was turned around by changes in the town he once knew. By matters of this day. By our unbelievable reality.

On sale, dress costs two hundred dollars. Place it on hold. Random thoughts pop in and out of my mind. Tony would love this dress. Tony would love that it came from this shop. Chuckle at the irony of it. Followed by, should money be an issue when a wife is about to bury her husband? Then I hear Tony. His words playing in my head. One of his many sayings. Proverbs from an everyman. "What's the cost of not?" Familiar words impacting most of our large purchases, possible experiences, and career choices. Forcing an opposite reality into family decision-making. Bringing heart into headiness.

A few days later in overly expensive dress, the cut glaring of only one season's style, Mom picking up cost, I begin the official final walk of our life together. Not together. Behind. Casket ahead. Shrouded in remembrance of Tony's baptism. Font gurgling. Echoing grace off marble floors. Telling of his death in life and his life in death. Sons surround me in brand new black and grey suits. My beloveds flanking me with arms entwined. Begin walk of a lifetime, of a life. Down aisle of rented church. Stepping off slowly. As if our participation makes this walk real. "Boys," I say between chokes and tears, "I sobbed down the aisle to marry your father. Now I'll sob down this aisle to say goodbye."

The first time I cried down a church aisle I was also wearing an expensive dress Mom bought. My arm entwined in my father's. Dad and I overcome at back of church by day's enormity. Photos almost humorous. As if I'm going away for a very long time. Sweet, really. I miss Dad on this new aisle walk. Miss him greatly during this time of despair and confusion. Always a calming presence in the face of anything. Having gone ahead to what comes next. Absent for me this day, but shepherding Tony into life after life instead.

I imagined possibility of doing this aisle walk with our sons in the distant future. Our lives following the course of research and observation. Me outliving Tony in a more natural trajectory of events. This walk when sons hit middle age. With families of their own trailing behind. Preparation leading my way down aisle. Because at our age things happen. Tony could have been diagnosed with something accompanied by a name. That scenario might have rendered us thankful as we knew death lingered soon. Our shared tears mixing into one final goodbye.

Not now though. Not this way. Not without saying goodbye. Not on vacation. Not by drowning. Not on such a lovely day. Not so soon. Not when future looked so bright.

This day, this walk, another one of tears. Upending our original intention. Tony and I planning a quiet twenty-first anniversary evening just us tonight. Life being too full and crazy for celebrating on actual day. Imagined it unfolding like this: me in a brand new, whimsical blue dress. Purchased day before he died. Tried on in little restaurant and shop we lunched in with our family. Modeled it. Knowing without words his approval. Meeting later in that same restaurant two people Tony introduced as "friends." Understanding after all these years as a therapist's wife these friends are clients. Smile. But really thinking ahead to dinner at our favorite, small restaurant downtown. Tony in short-sleeve linen shirt. Tucked out like a Filipino barong. My new dress fitting snugly. Tags off. Pressed. Perfumed. Perhaps taking a walk afterwards through city streets hand in hand. Meeting this same couple again last night at visitation. Me, dressed in black. Blue dress balled up. On floor of closet. Tags still on. Awaiting fate in light of my new reality.

Step off as music begins. Walk forward feeling heat of Ricky and Paul, my stone silent bookends. One dazed. Other holding it together. Me sobbing. Listen to Mary's words sung. Saying yes to God. To becoming mother of Jesus. Despite fear of unknown with only an angel guiding her. Words rising from heart into world. Wrapping anxiety in hope. "Do not be afraid."

No, today I bury my beloved. In a different dress with different connotations, different tears. Surrounded by people constituting our life together.

Impossible to eat at funeral luncheon. The smell of Filipino barbecue making most people hungry. People approach between dry swallows of food offering something: smile, hug, words, promises of future lunch dates, some of which never happen. Need to pee. Seems like a distant dream though. I've been standing next to our table for hours. Greeting grief, person by person. Finally walking over to thank neighbors, our caterers providing a bounty of lasagna. Thinking I can slip out next. Walk the cool narthex floors. Find the women's room. Relieve myself. Cornered again. By a fellow church member, one I do not know very well. Concern written all over her face. Not for my immediate needs. But for our horror. "We have all year to see each other," I say. "I'm not going anywhere. But right now, I just need to use the bathroom!"

Scare her for second time in less than twenty-four hours. At visitation, she clutched my hand saying, "God has a plan."

Blurt out: "God did not plan Tony's death! I will not minimize God with this theology!"

Words revealing intense need to protect my children from this thinking. God never planning ahead for the day which brings us to this moment. God's power in God's presence. Always. With Tony. With us. Today walking away from this well-meaning woman. Shaking. Finding brief moment of quiet. In stall. Of rented church. At my husband's funeral luncheon. Alone.

Car doors open for us. Driver, a funeral home person. Interior quiet. Used to holding pain. Cool air blasts away heat. Drive through winding roads of cemetery. Car doors open again for us. Walk down slight incline toward tent. Covering plot. Hiding hole. Hill giving women in heels or with some age a challenge. August hot in tent. No wind. Sweat through stiff clothing half-listening to prayers. Family placing a hand and flower on casket one by one. Saying final farewells. My mother-in-law chanting liturgy—what pieces I do not remember. Only her actions are beautiful.

My turn. Take one last walk with Tony, alone. Around his casket. Handmade of cherry wood. Same wood of our bedroom set. Casket built by monks north of here. Prayed over in the making. Tony's name marked forever in their books. Craftsmen producing what funeral director tells us days before is the only casket worth buying. Rest being junk. Ricky laughing. Having just told me privately the other caskets are crap or shit or something like that.

Walk around simple, handsome closed casket containing semblance of Tony's earthly beauty. Throwing rose petals. Buzzing bees and warm rustling leaves accompanying me. In absence of human sound. Allowing numb soul space to erupt. Into repetitious chant. "I love you," uttered as each petal takes flight. "I love you." In an act of public intimacy. "I love you." Until hands empty. Walk finished.

Limo weaves away. Leaving Tony. Leaving what once was. Traveling toward church. Collecting our things. Piling into Tony's old Mercedes. Ricky driving. Three of us winding through old streets avoiding summer construction. Traveling toward home, this day done. Unsure of what comes next. Life? Future? Making sense of what happened? Wondering how to live? Pray for endurance, fortitude, courage, tenacity, and hope. In this new walk. Without Tony. Carried forward by his words, "Jen, hope lives in the work of healing."

Survival Practice

Breathing: Place hand on heart. Breathe. Place hand on stomach. Breathe. Place one hand on heart and other hand on stomach. Close eyes. Breathe as best you can.[6]

Prayer

How, God? How?

Our wedding day, August 5, 1995.

The last photo of us together taken at Ricky's high school graduation in May 2016.

---

[6] Based on Peter A. Levine, *Healing Trauma: A Pioneering Program for Restoring the Wisdom of Your Body* (Boulder, CO: Sounds True, 2009), 68–69.

Tony's clinical practice was called The Men's Center. The logo shown here was designed by our niece, Marissa Panganiban.

Tony had a collection of wooden statues depicting pain and sorrow in The Men's Center.

II. Frozen Fall

"What would the observer say?"
—Tony Rodriguez

Before

Spring. Flowers poke out of loamy ground. Grass greens. Trees leaf out. In our home, we sniffle. Pop antihistamine. Drip in eye drops coating our puffy eyes with soothing substances.

May 2015. End of Ricky's junior year in high school and Paul's seventh grade year. Something shifts in our family's cohesiveness. Accumulating layers challenge our goodness and love as a family. Paul's just recovered from a series of anaphylactic reactions. Maybe from allergy shots. We don't really know. Went on for months. Allergy shots on Monday. Wednesday, flu-like symptoms. Fine again by the weekend. Cease shots, symptoms go away. A mystery. Not common. Feel relieved. Life returning to our normal. Until Paul orders a shake after a soccer tournament. Tells the fast-food employee of his peanut allergy. Drinks most of the shake. Looks at me funny saying, "Mom, what's this brown stuff?" Points to large peanut butter glob. Sitting in the bottom of his cup.

"Let's go," I say. Stop long enough to scream at employees. Race to emergency room. Paul flushing redder and redder. Even after giving himself a shot of epinephrine in the parking lot of the offending restaurant.

He recovers. But after months of Paul's collective reactions, my limbs hang limp. Work suffers. I frustrate easily. Feel jealous of Tony's ability to fly away each day to his office, while I stay home sprouting seeds of caregiver burnout.

Not catching my breath. For something else brews. A red, itchy rash covers Ricky from head to toe. Popping out of his scalp. Erupting on his stomach. Traveling up and down his arms. Ricky scratching constantly. Moving with anxiety. Demanding. Throwing me into a spin. The kind to which only the worn-out succumb.

Over the summer Paul rallies. Seems somewhat his old self. Ricky worsens. Places himself on a restrictive anti-inflammatory diet. Something he read about online. A dietary framework necessitating I prepare two different dinners each night. Tied to the kitchen for hours each evening.

Outside our home, vacant lot next door turns into complicated construction zone. Spilling over into our yard. Noise all day long. On the weekends, too. Construction men smoking in our drive. Yelling at our dog. Looking through our windows. Constant noise further impacting my ability to work, a freelancer from home office.

Thunder, our beloved dog, becomes more and more agitated. Speak with veterinarian. Gives me ideas to implement. Do so obediently. But really, no time to think about the dog. By fall, Ricky develops a weird grey color to his skin, loses lots of weight, and self-medicates. Numbing substances sold easily in the halls of his award-winning high school. School attendance scatters. He complains of not being able to read anymore. His reasoning like that of a much younger child. Words flowing from his mouth curse the world with vulgarity. The family room sofa becomes his home. Video games at all hours. Music continues on guitar and drums when his neck is not cramped up into a tight knot.

Tony out of town for further clinical training one weekend. Our dog Thunder bites a child while walking with Ricky, a walk I demanded in my own stress. Leaving me alone in our kitchen with a large, angry father bearing down on me with threats. Another doctor. Big. Iowa style.

Hell breaks loose. Neighbors file police complaints behind our backs. Same neighbors who in recent past sought my counsel about their aging parents. Now no courage to speak to us, face-to-face. Or sit with our ripping hearts. Trying to figure out if our beloved son is dying or not. Betrayal added to pain affixing to doctors and diseases with no names. From a group of seemingly nice white people. Alerting our family of color warning system. Tolling "be careful." Grateful for more compassionate neighbors calmly walking us through what needs to be done with our beloved dog.

Thunder put down. On a Wednesday night. Ricky making Thunder a steak for his last meal. Taking him for a walk in the woods near the lake. Asking why over and over and over again. Me, having no answers. Ricky and Tony caring for him at the end. Petting him. Saying goodbye. Holding him. Coming home in tears. Tears lasting for days. Me, quietly cleaning away Thunder's things. Ricky hanging Thunder's leash, the one Tony wove out of boat rope, on his bedroom wall. A photo on his nightstand. Parental prayers bouncing off all inanimate objects. "Please. Please God, may this death not plummet Ricky further down into this black hole."

Two weeks later Ricky's dear friend died of suicide, mental illness having the last say. Ricky finding out on my birthday. Subdued during dinner. Not telling us until Paul sees a message on the boys' shared computer. Asks Tony about it. Slowly unfolding a scene full of alcohol, favorite park, rope, and tree. Ricky and friends covering their lost friend's red truck with bouquets of flowers and notes. Tony and I knowing we can lose our son too. Thinking, how much can a young person take?

October onwards is stormy in our home. For Ricky. For us. Communication difficult. Words erupting into verbal fights, slammed doors. His emotions are those of a much younger child. We worry about Paul. Bearing witness to this mess we live. Still dealing with his own health. I worry about Tony. Especially Tony. His work emotionally draining. Our home currently not fulfilling or restful. Sleep's healing powers eluding us. Crying together in night's midst. Reaching for each other's hand. All the comfort we can muster day after day of feeling helpless. Desperate in our attempts to stay afloat. To breathe.

When sleep comes, new neighbor's smart home heating and air conditioning unit clanks and growls at high pitches regardless of the weather. Not like the typical air conditioning unit. No approximant, seasonal life span. Meaning silent in fall, winter, and early spring. This contraption revving up with gusto each night outside our bedroom window beginning in November. Fresh nightly air no longer a right. Our complaints met by puzzled looks. From owners not living in the house yet. Heating contractor minimizing our experience as if it is our problem. City manager in charge of permits nervous.

Ricky grows frustrated with steroid-based creams and lotions prescribed for his skin condition, which seems something other than eczema. But each doctor we visit calls his all-body skin inflammation by another name meaning the same thing. "Atopic dermatitis," they pronounce.

Some showing compassion through caring eyes. Many shrugging shoulders. Moving on to next patient. Practicing medical disassociation. Ricky railing in the car, "I just can't use steroid creams the rest of my life!"

Turning over every rock looking for answers. Often sidetracked by drug paraphernalia found in Ricky's bedroom. Smells remembered from college collecting in corners of our home. Not understanding how. Spinning. Restless. Tony finally saying, "You can't see the real cause if you keep focusing on the drugs."

His calmness is irritating. As if whatever this is will pass. I ask Tony to find me a therapist. I am in burnout. Need help, now. Tony suggests Marit. I dump on her, week after week.

Clicking away, Ricky types. Fingers flying at computer day after day. Looking for answers. Asking for this new diet, nutritional supplement, or medical test. His friends researching too.

Tony keeping our income flowing. Me heading project "Get Ricky Well." We see several specialists at the University of Iowa. The allergist laughing, saying, "You are a strong young man. Learn to live with this."

Afterwards walking back to parking ramp dejected. Deflated.

Make three or four visits to Mayo Clinic in Rochester, Minnesota. With nothing to show for our efforts. Wonderful doctors stumped by this skinny, smelly, stringy-haired kid wearing clothes he slept in asking highly articulate, well-researched questions.

About the same time Paul is again laid up and out of school for weeks. Living on the living room sofa. Miserable with flu-like symptoms. Until we see a post-doc at the university hospital. Born across the ocean. In a country knowing need. Understanding firsthand what infections looks like. Not needing a medical text to teach him symptomology. "This is c-diff," he tells me. The test confirms days later what this man already knows.

Ricky then insists we travel to a tiny town between Willmar and St. Cloud, Minnesota. To see a functional medicine doctor. Me relenting because, well, we are desperate. Willing in our collective disheartenment to pay out of pocket. Calling several times only to be put on a very long waiting list. Calling again one day at Ricky's urging. Adding more guilt to my motherly misery. Gulping when the scheduler says we can be seen in just a few weeks' time. Making appointments for both sons since Paul's health seems compromised from his series of odd illnesses.

Doctor visit in June bringing small shard of hope. CDC verifiable Lyme disease for Ricky. Tricky to treat. Running rampant in his body for so many months, possibly years. Inflaming his joints and brain. Paul, still a mystery. But treatment available for Ricky. Worthy of beginning. Graced now with a point of direction. Off in the horizon. Next point visible in the distance. A follow-up doctor's appointment in a few short weeks. Showing us a way out of this mess.

Antibiotics packed. Car loaded. Claiming a small act of respite for ourselves. A four-day weekend away from doctors, neighbors, and clanking machines. We head off to Spring Green, Wisconsin. Traveling tandem with my mother, brother Peter, and his two young daughters. To a small, pastoral place Tony loved. Where he reveled in small shops, rolling green pastures, and air heavy with nature. Second night there, the night before Tony's life force left us, left his body, Tony gives Ricky a stern lecture. "You must take your medications every day!"

Me, shushing them for the sake of the sleeping household. Tony shushing me for the first time in our life together. Continuing his teaching. Giving a gift. Ricky listening.

Week Two

Stagger under weight. Pound added to pounds. Like watching a brick layer construct a wall upon my soul. Brick by brick. Slimy grit adhering. Gathering new height. Building up. Walling me in. God, how much more can we take? Bedroom walls receiving wails. At night. Alone. Aware Tony no longer takes up space. With his smile, snores, sighs. Mumbled, sleepy words. Rhythmic breathing. Throat clearing. Whispers as if we still tiptoe around a sleeping baby. Shared laughter. Spoken and silent disagreements.

Paul hiding in sleep or screen. As if he never crawled out of his sleeping bag. The one he crawled into after the beach. Barely functioning. Nothing to look forward to. Ricky out. Hiding in other ways. Going to college right now not an option between illness and death. Looking for a job. One fitting his hours. Up all night. Asleep all day.

Child development training nudges me with truths. Even emotionally stable families falter and fall under too many stressors. Human beings crumple under life's weighty existence. Resilient families fare better, sometimes. No guarantee. Maybe ours? Led now in unwanted reality by solo parent? Two months ago, excelling in psychological evaluation. Tests required for seminary. My former me. Now? Doubting my courage and abilities. Weakened internal, emotional structures. Under weight of this shit, crap, beyond awfulness forcing down our family inside and out. Straining all Tony and I built. Culminating in death. Sudden, unnecessary, traumatizing death spread over our already solidified layers of pain. Collective hurts constructed before Tony died. Built over eighteen months of hell. Erected on top of goodness created over two decades. Anguish swaying our carefully laid and loved structure. Pray for mercy. The only way I remember how. "Kyrie eleison, Christe eleison, Kyrie eleison. Amen."

Toilet Talk

Late August. Everyone goes home. Leaving us in empty, eerie silence. Manage to clog toilet, even though eating is more conceptual than reality for me. Pick up plunger. Stare at loose mess of feces, urine, and shredded toilet paper. Too tired to curse or groan.

Plunging does not work. Walk downstairs to storage room. Rummage through cans of half-used paint, drill bits of every size and shape, and multitudes of IKEA instruction manuals. Uncover three toilet snakes. Haul them up to our bathroom. Drop snakes on cool tile floor. Collapse in bed. Exhausted.

Next few days ignore problem. Possible action paralyzing me. No idea how to use snakes. No ability to learn in early grief mixed with trauma. Barely accomplish what I already know how to do. Other day tried filling up car with gas. Arms shaking. Holding pump saying, "You know how to do this. You can do this." Afterwards tentatively driving home to safety. Wide world now full of unknowns.

Tell a friend. Sends husband over. Gunnar arrives after another dinner not eaten. Carrying his own plunger. People bring their own plungers? Don't you use the house plunger?

"Problem needs snake not plunger," I say as if I know.

"Nope," he says inserting plunger in toilet. "Spent a couple of years working as a camp counselor. Did a lot of plunging."

Gunnar works as if using plunger like brushing one's teeth, a twice daily occurrence. Tony's plunging much slower. Always accompanied by fake curse words, heavy breathing, and a look of disgust. Gunnar doesn't seem to mind looking at someone else's old feces. Watch as doorframe holds me up. Giving me an escape route out of master bath if needed. The one I think too big. Tony insisting could not be smaller. Begin trembling. Trauma's adrenaline speeding through body. Sorrow through heart.

Am learning that profound grief rises at odd moments. Like dinnertime when the garage door motor should purr announcing Tony's return to us. Like at noon when I might actually get ahold of him at work. Like in the middle of the night, when his warmth next to mine soothes me. But Tony isn't merely out of the country or at a conference. Me calling on a good friend for help. No, this moment? Mine alone. Recently rendered husbandless by freakishness. By a municipality's unforgivable lack of safety measures. Instead, talking with a different man in our bathroom. Understanding Tony would not like this scene at all. Me with another man. In closeness of our shared bathroom. Small bits of healthy jealousy flashing across his face. Kind which turned my lips upward not long ago. Reminding me of our attachment. Full of love and still a bit of lust.

Mind runs away. Body freezes to door frame. Gunnar's plunging shakes the glass shelf. One above toilet. Rattling row of perfume bottles. Glass shaking on glass. Gunnar's head jerking up. Knocking glass shelf. Newest perfume bottle hits tile floor. Shatters. Scattering glass everywhere. Odor rising. Making our bathroom smell like a lemon juicer on this hot, humid, August day. Silence follows before sputtering apologies begin.

Just days after Tony's death, learn my brother and his wife plan separation. Janice, my sister-in-law, flies from Germany for funeral. Hands me a gift, a bottle of lemon perfume. People bring cards, flowers, food. What will I do with a bottle of lemon perfume? Wear it in my state of mourning? Apply before fancy parties or receptions I will not attend? Trigger my asthma? Glass shards shatter one less oddity needing comprehension in current cutting reality.

Gunnar embarrassed. Not quietly either. Being a man of words, an academic. My rawness takes emotional precedence, however. I do not care about others' responses to anything. Gloss over incident as we clean up. Needing to leave our bathroom for emotionally safer ground. But Gunnar closes toilet lid. Sits down. What's he doing? I lean again against door frame. "I don't know how to help you right now. Glad to fix your toilet. Actually do something for you."

Listen through layers of despair. Accepting family and friends bumbling on tragedy's periphery.

Until I stiffen. Realizing as Gunnar talks, his view from our toilet seat lines up with a pair of my panties. Hanging on hook near door having come out of dryer a bit damp. Never occurring to me that someone other than myself or Tony or maybe my mother might see my underwear.

Tony worked with sex offenders involved with judicial court system early in our marriage. Every night made sure we closed our shades so no one could peer in. Like the local peeping Tom progressing toward becoming sexually violent. Even running out to get newspaper in my pajamas and robe forbidden. "It's an invitation," Tony said.

Tony cooling over the years. Me, embracing his knowledge base more. Now feeling stupid. Shame heating face. Wondering what to do. Having no energy for this socially uncomfortable moment. Or anything, really. Gunnar oblivious. Talking away. My mortification making sense. This other part not. Except it should be Tony talking with me. Appreciating my panties.

And that's it, isn't it? If Tony lived, somehow surviving that treacherous day, this room would still be our shared bathroom.

Tony sitting on the chair, the one next to towel bar, telling me of his day while I brush my teeth. Me saying let's continue talking in bed. But finding him asleep by the time I get there. Mornings hearing him sing in the shower. Talking to each other through steam. Grumbling over toilet lid cover taken off again. Because we had a kind of war going on over it.

Tell Gunnar's wife Abbey about panties. Laugh a long time like girls on a sleepover talking about boys. Cooling my intense emotions. Creating a grief break of sorts. Wonder together whether or not to tell Gunnar. Elect to keep him innocent.

Advent creeps in late November. Abbey gives me a prayer. Tape it to bathroom mirror. On Tony's side of the commode. "Holy One, thank you for the story that begins here…"

Prayers for Me and My People

Warm September day. Sitting outside in a small Iowa town with a grain elevator and an active main street. Sarie, my pastor friend, and I lunch. Talking for hours in shaded sunshine of fall. Bees buzzing aiming for our food. Me wondering aloud if I like the prayers other people pray for us now. Words prayed freely. Lamented in our stead. Because I struggle to pray right now. Words bypassing heart. Roadblocked in head leading to my lips. People stepping in. Taking over prayer life like they've taken over our home and food. "Don't I get a say in what people pray for us?"

Sarie assessing my words. As a woman, pastor, someone knowing loss. Nodding. "Of course you do."

"Maybe I should write my own," I say.

Later I write, God of love and healing, bring Ricky, Paul, and I together during this time of intense trial. Mend what is broken in our relationships and build on what is already strong. Remind us to seek each other out when we need to openly grieve or remember Dad and husband even when we think being alone is safer.

Show us new ways of feeling Tony's love for us and learning from his knowledge of humanity. Help us discover our vulnerabilities during these days of mourning so that our vulnerabilities lead us to true courage and courage to hope for the future.

Tony's death creates a new and large hole in our lives. Help us fill this hole with all that Tony wished for us—love, meaningful work, supportive friends and family, people with generous spirits, good health, zest for living, and the courage to face life each day and night with hope and tenacity.

Show us ways to heal our broken hearts, dear Lord, each in the ways we need best. Assure us that our brokenness is not what drives our future but what makes us human. Calm our anxieties, our ghosts, and our intense emotions surrounding Tony's death. Show us the light every day no matter how dim and far away leading us back to a newfound wholeness on earth and in doing so repeating again and again that we do best walking toward life and away from death.

Make learning, work, and school safe harbors of self-discovery for all of us in our healing journey as we learn who we are without Tony's physical presence in our lives. May the uncomfortableness inherent in learning be in its own way a balm in the reformation of our lives.

Keep us on a true track of healing, avoiding unhealthy escapist or numbing behaviors which only prolong and worsen our plights. Instead teach us new ways to cope with, understand, and welcome the hard work of healing and the insight that the long road of healing is the quickest route to rebuilding our lives, recreating our dreams, and reaching for them.

Surround us with the light, love, and warmth of friends and family. May these people bolster us when we struggle with grief's weight in the painful hours of our days.

Gracious God, hold us with gentleness in all that we pray. Fill in the gaps of what we ask knowing what we do not know or need. Grow your Spirit within us so that one day you may use us again as instruments of love, peace, and compassion. We ask all these things in your name, Amen.

Journal Entry

Almost One Month: 2:24 a.m.

Up. Ricky wanting, needing parenting. Me needing to give it. He now settled. Me wide awake, arms aching. Remembering it's almost one month now.

9:54 p.m.

Mail today brought a package of religious tracts. Sender unknown. From a Roman Catholic source in Wisconsin. Persuading me to walk away from seminary. Messages cut. Deepening my bleeding wounds. Rail at another injustice cloaked in crap. Write to unknown senders an unsent letter.

Face ME. Look ME in the eye. See ME. Hear ME. You, sending words thinking you are right. You, sitting in judgement of my trauma and my grief. You, hiding from me. You, fearing me.

You send hate where others send love. You send disturbance where others send balm.

You want to wound. Others want to heal. Hate me. Hate me in God's name and wonder why God won't sign God's name to your ploy. Only other humans who forget their own humanity. I haven't forgotten mine. I cannot forget in my suffering while bearing witness to my children's suffering, can I? You live in a luxury I cannot have. But like the Romans, luxury may kill you.

Moaning Molecules

Body aches. Without your proximity. Here. Remembering dancing arm and arm in kitchen. Warmth of your hand on my back. Bodies moving in tandem. My body smelling you when apart. Separated by a wall, a floor, a ceiling, a few miles. Even split by states, you in one and me in the other. Our human produced chemicals circling between distances. Awaiting reunion. Moving in this knowing. Yearning to dance. Only you don't return. My molecules searching. Searching for yours. Moaning. Aching in the night, day. Calling you back. My throbbing molecules pining for yours.

Journal Entries

Eve of One Month: 9:45 p.m.

Sleep eludes me. Noise wakes me. Worry besets me. Tears take me. We are enough just us, I have to think so. I can't fill this empty space Tony leaves unwillingly. Want to fill it. With what I do not know. Hurried grief does not heal—at least I do not think so. Having watched others try. Fail. Grieve even more. Old feelings emerge from before Tony. Loneliness. Feeling lost. In New York City. In Chicago. Not as alone now. Have two sons. Am I destined to spend so much time without a partner? Think this thought is shame showing its evil self once again. As part of this unasked for journey.

One Month and Four Days: 12:10 a.m.

Things I wish I had told Tony before he died.
1. I love you
2. Thank you for our life together
3. Thank you for wanting and being a good father to our beloved sons, Paul & Ricky
4. Thank you for our sons
5. You took me on an incredible journey, one I didn't always want to be on. I'm not a risk taker but we took a risk in The Men's Center and because we did, people's lives changed. I treasure this knowledge of how you healed so many people
6. I wish you had told me about the accumulated boxes at the center taking over and had asked me to help you
7. I treasure our morning trip to St. Cloud, Minnesota. Just us having fun trying out cars in the early morning

8. We didn't always agree on the small stuff of life but we did on the big stuff
9. I didn't know how many lives you touched. I just didn't know. In that way I wish you had been less humble even though I always admired your humility and wished I had more of it
10. I love you. I will always love you

Fears

Just after midnight. Staring into night again. Aware of energy working up and down arms. Arms holding fear. So many fears. Fear creating fear. Flick on light. Give in to open eyes, spinning head, aching heart. Sit up. Find journal. Click pen. Fears flow creeping down arms awakening fingers. Feeding pen. Igniting movements into words.

Name fears. Trepidation by trepidation. Ending with possible horror, another one. Ancient knowledge fossilized within me. Within all women. Dead yet alive with seeds ready to sprout again. As if this trauma, the trauma of the ages, lives in a perpetual season of human spring. Causing a collective dread by all women victimized by men. Only not talked about enough, women to women. Women to men. Women to humans. Instead hid under cloak of shame. Oozing out from cape's folds as women shame women after men begin the process. Repeated so often, the shame, fear, and nightmare is always alive. Never dormant. Ready to pounce like a predator on weakened prey. "Are you safe enough?" Tony asks.

"I don't know," I reply. Begin writing.

Things that scare me.

1. Parenting Ricky and Paul alone
2. Paul's high school years
3. Paul & Ricky avoiding hard work of healing
4. Not having enough money
5. Not having meaningful work

6. Not going to seminary
7. Taking care of everything
8. Losing anyone else especially one of the boys
9. The rest of my life. The rest of my life scares me
10. Not selling The Men's Center
11. Not enough life insurance
12. Being dropped like a lead balloon by Tony's parents and Tita, the family's matriarch
13. Wondering what to do every weekend
14. Being asked to do things with other yet older widows
15. Feeling crappy all the time
16. Having to grieve and heal and parent all at the same time
17. Getting sick and needing to be taken care of
18. Getting sick now while boys still at home
19. Dying young
20. Being forgotten by others
21. Being alone once the boys go away to school and beyond
22. Not reading people well—always had Tony to do that for me
23. Being preyed upon

Incomprehension

Light brown sand. Fine and plentiful. Sinks beneath toes just a fraction. Adjusting to feet's weight. Swirls of cool water break at ankles. Clouds above hang from August blue sky. Boat motors purr. A group of people tubing floats by. Children laugh. People chatter. Hum pleases my ears.

Water takes kayak easily from my hands. Increase grip on short rope separating me from my niece, happy in our orange boat. Lifetime spent on Midwestern waterways automates my responses to the water. But brain works much more slowly. Something doesn't make sense with this water. With this day. Beach, full of sunbathers and waders. Water, full of boats. Scene, full of happiness.

I glance. Glance again. Again. Tony, Ricky, Paul seem too far out in the river. But other people are out there as well. Boaters just feet away from them. Yet the clear water swirling at my feet pulls with insistence.

Glance again. How many times do I glance? Before the world stops time. Before my body begins its slow-motion march toward my beloveds. Before I feel the relief of seeing Paul and Ricky emerge into shallow water and onto the sand. Different than the two carefree teenagers who went in. Slow. Wooden. Silent except for Ricky's low voice robotically saying, "Dad's in trouble."

Continue walking. Toward Tony. Water circling me in fierceness. Up to waist. Then chest. Life jacket bobbing at neck. Walking. Toward my Tony. Toward my love. Toward my life. Stopping when he disappears under the water.

Accidental Death

The day before Tony died rain pelted down for hours. We threw on raincoats, ponchos, mukluks. Trudged through woods toward farm pond. Fished in rain off the dock or in a small dingy. Warning, like all good parents, to remain seated in the boat and wear your life vests. Until our children stopped listening. By evening rain letting up. Piled into two cars. Headed for an outdoor theatre. Watched a Shakespeare comedy. Don't remember which one. In our car just our small family clan. Four of us driving to and from the theatre. Quiet. Calm. Thinking, *this is who we are as a family.*

Alarm strikes like bullets each time I find Paul staring at photo of the beach. Taken from bridge. Posted on computer. Called Peck's Landing. Paul stares. Crying at times. Other times just slumped in sadness.

Wonder what it was like for my father to return to the farm. Growing up, we didn't visit often. But enough to catch grief lingering in the air. Sadness swirling along with gratitude of hungry settlers looking for a better life. Land holding pain of those who were there before them. People with whom they exchanged bread for venison. Who eventually moved on without words. Leaving their sorrow in the land one step at a time. My people, relieved yet guilty. Living on creating happy memories filled with story and laughter. Fending off gnawing of missed loved ones, feverish brow of child, at times hunger, and wretched memories stuck against an outbuilding marking death.

A friend stays with us over the long Labor Day weekend. We drive to a cutting garden outside of town. On a farm raising beef cattle. We collect flowers for Tony's grave. Watch farmer stand in pen with cattle and snorting bull. Bull's massive body heaving. Charging. No warning. Farmer calling out. Sort of like a "heads up" only in cattle raising lexicon. Bull making loud noises unknown to me. Scary sounds from a scary beast.

At once I see the scene known only through cells connecting me to my ancestors and family lore. Or perhaps as a tag on my DNA as the epigeneticists talk of. My grandfather walks into the bull pen. Bull snorts. Charges. Pins Carl against the barn with his horns. Bull releases. Carl slumps. Who helps him from the pen, across the yard, and into the house, I do not know.

He rests on the daybed in the front room. Later sits in the family rocking chair. Next morning the ten-year-old boy who will one day be my father nags him about something before school. Carl dies later that day in that same rocking chair. From bull's force. A farm accident, one of many out on the prairies. Death caused by one wrong move. By unforeseen circumstances.

What then do I teach my sons about nature and human responsibility now? Our careful lessons over the years filled the air. "Keep the fire pit at least twenty feet from the house. And never leave a fire unattended. Douse the embers with water at the end of the night. Learn to swim and swim well. Wear reflective clothing when biking. Have a light on in the boat for dusk and night. Get off the water when thunder begins rolling in. If you tip the kayak, right it from underneath. Never kayak in a spring river."

Morels

There they sit, blanketed in fallen oak leaves of lonely fall. Off to the left of the wood's path. Poking out as if to say, "Here we are!"

I stop. Trying to comprehend this sight. The season passed months ago for mushrooms of such coveted delicacy. But these two, side by side, one taller than the other, seem happy. Like naughty children, almost. Making a joke of weather's continued unseasonable temperatures.

Our first May together, Tony and I traveled from Chicago to Manistee, Michigan. Spent a few days with my parents. Went morel mushroom hunting in forests surrounding their cabin. Hunted and hunted with no luck. Failures in foraging for our dinner. "There's one!"

Tony's cry echoing off trees. City boy spotting one hiding. Pride carries Tony back to the cabin.

My father, forgetting his manners. "I've just plummeted," he said.

Tony laughing. These two bonding. My father towering over Tony in Nordic height as they smiled at each other. Began a good friendship. Standing together now, I think. Beside my path. Reminding me of our mushroom hunt twenty-one years ago. Wishing me happy birthday on this sad, sad day. Telling me they are together. Somewhere. All is well. Watching over me. Holding me as best they can through earth and sky. Next to my new path this day. Without either of them here.

No Goodbye

How do I say "goodbye?"
                    —Journal entry, close to three months after

Real horror of sudden and unexpected death. Words not said, last words remembered as not enough, wondering what last utterances really meant, second guessing it all. Creating closure alone. Pretending Tony present. Talking to him in therapist's office. Therapist saying, "Tell him you love him."

Writing Tony a letter before burning it. Smoke taking sentiments toward heaven or sky or further into God. Ashes adding to rubble left to clean up. After people return home to their own lives. Leave the unclosed at our home. Which feels not ours now. House full of well-meaning leftover food, remnants of Tony's life until recently lived, reminders of what was and now isn't, and internal debris of a relationship no longer physically present. But ever so stuck within me in this wilderness of emotional unknowns.

Our last goodbye, a silent exchange across a row of seats full of our people. Eyes meeting. Tony blinking. Me returning a half-smile. He nodding. An exchange of love, history, relationship, commitment. Last moment. Final words lost in everyday exchanges.

Cleaning Out

Force visit to Tony's office. With sons. Just three of us. Entryway dusty from street construction. Walk up creaky, steep steps. Old kind going up and up. Gloomy hallway despite skylight above. Reach landing. Hands sweat, shake unlocking door. The one marked, The Men's Center. Enter waiting room. Stomach lurches. Ricky turns on lamps. Ones used for relaxing, ambient lighting. Tony hated fluorescents.

To the right, August sun shines through bank of windows spanning entire office wall. Walk toward light, into Tony's large office. Desk left as if owner returning any moment from lunch. Accent pillows scattered on gold couch. Framed art adorning walls. Book shelves full, lining one entire wall. Office, a living room. The therapeutic point of the place.

"I need to find the life insurance policy."

Paw papers on desk. Open mail. Look through file folders. Policy could be anywhere. "Why isn't it in the safety deposit box where it should be?"

Unlock file room. Large, metal cabinets stare. Capable of harm. Mostly full of client files. Where are the business files? Not well enough to think cognitively. Make a game of sorts. Wonder aloud, "Now if I were Tony, where would I keep...?" Death's aftermath not a game. When did I lose track of this type of stuff?

We don't stay long.

Stay away for a good week. Forced to return. Sole owner of business needing tending. Enter space wearing black. Putting world on notice of my pain. Reminding those already forgetting.

Make cold call to another therapist interested in expanding. Meet his business manager in Tony's office. Reject him. No energy for negotiation games. Ones he excels in. Feel in my gut these men want a version of The Men's Center capable of pummeling my beat-up soul.

Continue making sense of the center. Office in better shape than expected. Tony turning a new organizational leaf with help of administrative assistants, Ricky being one of them. Still, the storage room overflows with boxes and old office equipment. Every few days dump another dusty box onto floor of office. Kneel in its contents ranting at Tony. Screaming at universe's brutality. Anger at business left to me. Telling Pastor Peter, "the man never opened a piece of mail in twelve years!"

Peter chuckles at other end of phone. "You don't open your mail either, do you?" I say.

He doesn't reply.

Stand in chaos, not love. Just want Tony back. Seeing clients. Ushering couples into his office. Asking, "How are ya today?" His soft tones warming the space. Soothing even the addictions. Opening all up for healing. Voice, no longer present here. Gone in real time. In shock cannot access memory of its timbre and lilt.

Call insurance company. Have no idea what to live on except maybe the memorial money or my mother's generous checks, or some savings tucked away in mutual funds with no easy access. Waiting follows. No information shared over phone. Letter from insurance company informing me payout takes three weeks. Person doing these letters on vacation.

Learn more things about work required post-death. Credit cards in Tony's name alone not my responsibility. Cutting potential business bills quite a bit. Most owed businesses are kind. Know there will be a wait. Others not, person in letter or on other end of phone clueless as to shock's fog I push through each day. In my forced and ugly reality. Speaking with people daily who don't know what to say. Hiding behind hollow, rote phrases learned in training. Me setting them straight. One day they too will grieve. One afternoon break down screaming into the phone, "Do you have any idea what this is like for me?"

Pulling back creditor says, "I lost my father recently. I understand."

Close out a bank account for money to live on until insurance checks arrive. Not knowing how to pay for life while waiting. Insurance requiring many phone calls, letters, and paperwork. Need accident report, sheriff's report, and coroner's. Call Wisconsin. Ask for information I do not want. Wait for mail. Touching envelopes and contents as if contaminated. Transferring documents without looking at them to other envelopes. Addressed to those with financial power over me.

Another glitch. Insurance company cannot read Tony's handwriting. Therefore no legal beneficiary. Tony's penmanship an issue again. Like the love poems he sent when courting. Left unread but cherished. Beautiful, scripted, visually poetic words. Pen strokes communicating love through movement, not readable words. His signature, always a thing of beauty. But not legally binding right now. My lawyer steps in. First insurance check arrives in October, two months after Tony's death. Dwindles upon deposit into mounting bills spilling over into yet another office mess. Find life insurance policy months later. In unmarked box full of unfiled papers. Last box opened.

Wander around home straightening up. In high-pitched nervousness combined with fatigue. Needing a sense of order, safety in our chaos. Remember Mom cleaning out closets after Dad's cancer diagnosis. Looked like denial in my younger years. Now doing same thing. Clearing out as if Tony's death needs cleansing from me and from us in repeated acts of purification. In truth, it's a trauma reaction. Socially acceptable to others.

Clean out food. Arriving in bulk within twenty-four hours of Tony's death. Door bell ringing. Sons hiding. Me answering, playing hostess to our grief. Well-meaning others offering something concrete, life-sustaining. With a side of fumbled words. Continuing for ten weeks. Accumulating cases of flavored, carbonated water, pans of lasagna, crock pots of pulled pork, meat loaves meant for a threshing crew, stews of all sorts—vegetarian, spicy, beef, cooked ground beef slightly seasoned for throwing in spaghetti sauce for a quick meal, more lasagna, cut up vegetables with small and large containers of dip and dressing, everyone's extra garden produce especially tomatoes, zucchinis, and peppers, various baskets of fruit—apples, bananas, grapes, and oranges—brownies, bars, cookies, ice cream, assorted breads, bags of chips, boxes of crackers, homemade soups—chicken noodle, beef and barley, tomato basil, white bean Italian sausage—homemade berry pies, freezer meals barely glanced at but stuffed in, even more lasagna. Nonfood items as well. Mostly toilet paper, paper towels, tissues, eye drops, and twelve prayer shawls.

Received so much food that our main refrigerator, stuffed and stuffed some more, stopped working. Forcing Ricky and me to dump almost all the food. Followed by an old-fashioned defrosting. For exactly twenty-four hours. Ricky insisting. Detail oriented in this process. Taking charge during repairman's visit. Allowing me flight, away. To meet with women pastor friends. The ones keeping me breathing. Refrigerator defrosted by twenty-two hours. Beg to restock. "No mom, the repairman said twenty-four."

Chalk Ricky's behavior up to grief or medication working against insidious Lyme disease with brain inflammation. Hold tongue. Tie hands. Watch clock.

Another day Linnea and Tom drive over from Davenport, Iowa. Tom replaces cracked toilet seats and hangs pictures still stored from move five years ago. Centers one across from our bed. Flowered still life in vivid yellows, greens, purple, and orange. Something of beauty to gaze upon. Filling empty bedroom with color.

Linnea and I walk into our closet. Clean out Tony's ratty T-shirts. Ones boys not interested in. Decide Tony's trousers are already too short for our tall children. Begin piling trouser after trouser on bed. Linnea counting. Commenting, "Tony was such a good dresser."

Bring out last pile. Funny look crosses Linnea's face. "Jen, Tony had almost one hundred pairs of pants!"

Maybe I nod. Laugh. Exchange looks with another longtime wife. Both learning years ago to love our spouses along with their undefinable idiosyncrasies. Discovery today not a surprise. Married a man owning seven leather coats. Counted them one day in hall closet of his apartment. "Why do you need so many coats?"

"Gifts," Tony answered.

Learned Tony bought in multiple. Practiced retail repetition. Not one jug of antifreeze kept on hand but six. Not one cold remedy but ten. Funny thing about trousers. He only wore five pair of them. Over and over again. Save my favorite pair from pile. Load up Linnea's car with whatever these ninety-nine pairs of beautiful trousers represent for me or did for Tony. Watch one less load bearing down on heart wind away. Creating space in my head.

Ricky does this cleaning out ritual on his own. Loving Buddhist sense of simplicity. Paul too pours items into ever-growing garage pile of stuff slated for Salvation Army or Goodwill. In his case things no longer fitting even though they did a month ago.

Turn away from cleaning out Tony's things. Clean out mine instead. Make way for incoming products from aggressive retail therapy sessions. Bought online in night's midst. Sitting in bed. Wrapped in one of the recently acquired prayer shawls.

Shopping after listening to meditation app. Always choosing male guides. Longing for man's timbre. Shopping after last breath sent out with finally gong. Scouring sites for black, widowed wardrobe dresses. Adding color after three months. First dark hues. Gently layering in more vibrant shades. Reverting to black when feeling demand for widow's protectant. Reminding world of rawness. Buying in total eighteen dresses, four pairs of black or dark grey shoes—clogs, sandals, ankle boots, Keds—three or four pairs of trousers, two pairs of shorts, three blouses, two sweaters, jean jacket, two purses, six bras, necklace, two sets of pajamas in organic cotton, winter jacket bought with my mother. Mine black. Mom's burgundy. Two swimsuits, one dark navy to fit my widowhood. The other bright blues, greens, whites on a background of black.

More items bought daily, returned weekly. A perpetual cycle. Dissipating over time. Yet remaining prone to them when highly agitated. Needing endorphins. Especially when companies offer free shipping and returns. By winter, sporting the most updated wardrobe since college. Adult years always marked by fund shortages. Due to being in the arts, graduate school, student loan debt, having babies, opening a business, being too busy to bother. At a dinner party one night a friend says, "I want to study clothes shopping with you."

Better than studying grief with me, I think.

Setting Sun

Fall continues warm and dry. Harvest coating our small world with corn dust. Combines working into dark with headlights on. Bringing year's harvest in. Nearby grain dryers working day and night. Motor sounds floating across night sky. Entering open windows. Air's dryness creating large, expansive sunsets in reds, pinks, golds, and blues. Reaching into infinity. Colors keeping company with my walking steps each evening. Accompanying me like Tony did. Only without his hand in mine.

Breath fills what is left of my lungs. Measured inhale on the count of five. Exhaled the same. Over and over again. Repetition calming. Just enough to keep living.

Journal Entries

November 26, 2016.

Screamed at Ricky yesterday. Why I screamed fades quickly away. Scenes from our life disappearing like clouds on a windy day. Leaving feelings of unworthiness. Not enough in my son's eyes. He attacking. Me, attacking back. Throwing disparaging words about Tony into the air. Anger leading me. Trying so hard to remember Tony in love-infused phrases. Shying away from his true humanness. Not in this moment. Ricky backing down. In therapy, I tell Marit about words I am ashamed of. Before saying, "Maybe the boys have permission to remember all of Tony now. Take him down from his death pedestal."

Marit nods. Hard to tell what she thinks.

Final days before moving out of The Men's Center. Sit on floor day in, day out. Surrounded by dust, boxes, memories, tears. Watch one Sunday afternoon as box after box of client files leaves office door. Heading for legally mandated housing elsewhere. Guts of strangers once honored here. Our dreams flying away. My heart breaking again.

Friend in university's psychology doctoral program takes some of Tony's professional library. Shows me how many books are autographed. Surprises me into inaction. Easily done in my state. Too late to withdraw gift. Embracing instead work of new healer. As others once did for Tony. Paul rails at me for giving so much of Tony's library away. "How will I know?" he asks, "How will I know about stuff and protecting myself?"

He means protecting himself from sexual predators. Prime target at age at fourteen. Protection limited without a father. Both knowing this stuff. Awful tragic verity inherent in our situation. More vulnerable alone. Have no answer for Paul. Know I must be on guard for him, for me.

November 29, 2016.

Moving out of The Men's Center is hard for us all. A second death. But I cannot say this to Ricky and Paul. Dreamed of Tony last night. Do not remember dream. Except when I woke I knew he was not here and that somehow the dream had it wrong. My friend Sarie says grief and hope can exist at one time. Can I grieve Tony and hope for my future? Can my children do this? So many layers to this time. So many layers.

November 30, 2016.

Moving day. Full of sadness, deep sadness. Molecular and muscle sadness. Another leaving. Of a place where Tony gave so much to the world. By choice. By sacrificing his own needs. I loved Tony. It wasn't perfect, that is for sure. But it was real love. Loving each other "despite and still" as the poet Robert Graves writes.[7] Pray, Dear God, bring balm to this day. Coat us with loving memories. Catapult us forward into embracing our future, our now, our past. Bring us together as family. Mend old and new wounds. Create more love between us and around us and in us. Amen.

---

[7] Robert Graves, "Despite and Still," as set by Samuel Barber. "Despite and Still," in *Collected Songs for High Voice* (New York, NY: G. Schirmer, 1980).

Closing Words

On a dark afternoon in early December we close Tony's office door for the last time. Ricky says, "It was a good run," reentering the office once more as if looking for something or someone he lost.

Stunned, I stand keys in hand. Ricky uttering same words I wrote my dying father sixteen years ago. Sentiment embracing love and life. Permission for all to go on.

Locking the door, I breathe. As usual, the hallway smells of old wood. Sounds from restaurant below waft up stairway. Other bubbled glass office doors warm the vestibule with inner light. The one I lock, Tony's door, dark. Soon new life will again illuminate this door. But not today. Not in this moment.

We descend steep stairs. Not looking back. We part on the street below. Night air smelling of impending snow. Ricky heading for his new college apartment with a load of things. Watch him go. Do not want to go home.

Twelve years ago in November, Tony and I opened The Men's Center. Tony's dream, his calling, to do this work. Began by opening his heart and skill set to male survivors of childhood sexual abuse. Grew into working with and for people suffering from sexual addictions. In those early days, we debated the tagline for the business for what seemed like forever. Finally settling on "a place for healing, mindfulness, and possibilities." Our niece Marissa created the beautiful and heartfelt logo and web page. We rented an office space near home and bought supplies.

Work began. As a family we often saw only the beginnings and endings of Tony's days. Beginnings, hurried moments for all of us preparing for our days of work and school. Day's end, an exhausted and quiet human being. Used up willingly in the work of healing. Telling corny jokes. Letting off steam if anyone would listen. Vacations not free from work for any of us. One year hiking in Arizona's Santa Catalina foothills, Tony saved a client's life on a cell phone with poor reception. Another year he spent hours on the phone planning his book, *Facing Heartbreak: Steps to Recovery for Partners of Sex Addicts*.

In the wake of his death, I can only imagine the healing occurring within the walls of Tony's various offices. Sons and I "bore witness," as Tony said, to so many stories told to us in person and through cards and letters after his death. So many lives changed and saved. Stories keeping me breathing during first month after his death. Stories reminding me our life together was not lived in vain even as I looked out over our deck every morning donned in widow's black wondering how the future could happen without him.

The week before closing this door for the last time, I gathered our sons, mom, and pastor in Tony's office. Saying goodbye to The Men's Center in now empty space. Place housing this dream already without its warmth and healing.

We stood in a circle in the middle of the office. Talked of vocation. Remembered Spirit-filled early days of the business. When I never knew how to pay for anything, yet there was always money. Then we prayed. Acknowledging the courage this business took to create and maintain. Reminding ourselves that this same courage helps us live now without Tony.

So, on this very snowy night during our first Christmastide without him, I pay tribute to the work Tony did. A vocation I supported. A calling that defined Tony and in many ways defined our family. Work we never witnessed. Healing happening in complete confidentiality. Work I could at times resent. But work of which I was and still am in awe. A life's commitment which will always be to me and our sons synonymous with Tony's very being. His soul made more fully known to the world than most through his courage and sacrifice.

It was a good run, my darling. It was a very good run.

Survival Practice

Journal: Find, buy, ask for a journal. You don't even have to open it. You can just look at it. But keep it close by. Write in it if you need to.

Prayer

What next, God? What next?

Tony's parents' fiftieth wedding anniversary, 2010.

Thunder.

Tony's office showing his attention to the therapeutic environment at The Men's Center.

Tony was studying couple's therapy with Dr. Stan Tatkin. The chairs set up here show how couples faced each other during therapy, not the therapist.

III. Unbalanced Realities

"Do you want to feel better or do better? Because if you
want to do better, you have to do the work."
—Tony Rodriguez

Car Safety

Before Tony, Chicago's gray morning followed me. Driving south
on an almost empty Ashland Avenue. Protected from quiet world
by blaring music, closed windows, and metal frame. Lesson
plans, homemade play dough, and a jar of leftover minestrone
soup filled my bag. Smock dress covered my thin frame. Cassandra Wilson's velvet voice blanketed air. Soulfully singing, "Got to
find me an angel in my life."

Hit replay over and over again. Day after day. Same drive.
Same voice. Same prayer for filling my empty heart. On weekends, ride my bike along lake front. Feel a presence close. Felt
sense saying, "Do not worry. Do not be afraid."

Know my someone, my angel draws near. Proximate essence
haunting me for months on this ride. Often stop along path.
Gaze off into clouded horizon hovering over Lake Michigan. Others on bikes whizzing by me. Homeless men snoring on benches.
Children running in sand with wide smiles and happy shrieks.
Ride until universe shifts one day revealing my human angel.
Gentle, serious man living a mile or so north of me on Olive
Street between Clark and Glenwood. Who doesn't like Cassandra
Wilson much or any jazz for that matter. Not for another decade
or so. Prayer answered. Cassandra's cassette tapes gathering
dust in my car. Cast aside.

Lost my angel. Other music keeping me safe during this time. In different car after owning nine together. Morning drive under clear Iowa skies with smell of harvest in the air. Driving in silence. Until dropping Paul off at high school. "Have a good day. I love you," I say.

"Sure," he replies.

Pull car up a bit. Know Paul won't last long at school. Grief's time for overtaking me only a few short hours. Find CD, one from Tony's office. James Blunt's "Back to Bedlam." Remember how many times Tony sang his song "You're Beautiful" to one of us. Jokingly with the boys. Lovingly with me. Now bask, unwillingly, in many songs. Repeated with push of button. "Goodbye my lover. Goodbye my friend. You have been the one, you have been the one for me," sends tears shaking through every limb.

But "Tears and Rain" becomes one song to which my heart sticks. For months. Enveloping me with sound's sanctity. Fencing me off from world. Holding sorrow captive in melody and chordal progressions. Words not speaking to me. But sounds building over and over again. Opening a deep well. Producing deepest pain I've ever known. As Tony would say, "I'm in the pit."

Resistance

Can't write. Feel dried out from day's convulsing sobs and sighs. Writing, like other former basics, falls into abstraction becoming a concept aspired to rather than practiced. An absurd exercise when comprehending written word is like reading an unknown foreign language. Sudden grief and trauma's shock render me illiterate sending writing far away into another reality. Body contracts as each new, empty journal arrives via hands of friends. "I thought you might want to write," they say.

Why? I think. Why relive my pain in literary flashback?

Walk marshy grassland with Abbey one day. Fall sun cracking open milkweed pods. Butterflies drying wet wings. Air full of summer smells heading for winter. She asks, "Are you writing?"

Soul screams nooooooooo as gold finches flit among tall grasses. Bugs chirping in accompaniment. "I don't want to be that widow. You know the one documenting her sorrow like a scientist collecting data."

Abbey laughs. Maybe we both do. At my resistance to observing every nuance of living in existence's pit. Opening soul up in dishonorable literary discharge for others' to scrutinize.

Writing finds me once or twice a week regardless. In short journal entries or long traditional letters like ones grandmothers wrote and received. Handwritten on flowered dime-store stationery. Smelling of old lady perfume. Mine, love letters really to those holding us together during first days. Written in middle of night. Sitting up. Adjusting pillows. Reaching for lamp, paper, and pen. Words spinning through brain. Pushing until written down. Then evaporating. Words printed on beautiful pastel green or blue paper bought downtown at small stationery store. Sealed in envelopes with stamps. Placed in mailbox during early morning hours. Yesterday's black dress still clinging to body through restless night.

Not bothered by any of my nots. Not writing or eating or sleeping or breathing or reading. Not like others seem to be with their repeated questions and sometimes commands. My days, months, time, energy taken up by basic living like getting out of bed, parenting, after-death work, making sense of Tony's business, managing copious offers of help and food, reading daily influx of cards, texts, emails, and messages. Words written with love or containing sayings people murmur when horrified. Grieving when time. Although often untended as I host others in my own grief.

At three months, aware of certain post-death rhythm in all I do, do not do. Have accepted the adagio necessary for survival. In new rhythm stop counting weeks without Tony. Begin counting months. Add more nots to my list. Not cutting my hair. Allowing it to grow long and wild. Curl in humidity of warm fall and early snow. Not pretending to be kind to all who dare speak to me as if I am the me of before. Not wanting to give in to any of what happened to us. Resisting my heart's defeat.

Only sleep defies my litany of nots progressing to six hours most nights. Tossing coming at first light with maybe a brief fitful nap before rising. Dreams vacant. Until one early morning finding Tony in kitchen. Want to run, wake boys before he leaves. But he does leave. His face growing larger and larger. His smile taking up entire kitchen. Before vanishing again. Marit saying in therapy, "Tony wants to make sure you get the point."

"What point?"

"He loves you. He's okay."

Holding this knowledge, real or imagined, close. This love from beyond, however, not producing any energy. Small reserve leftover from before used for climbing out of muck each day into a far different and lonely world.

Brunch with my women friends in ministry group three months and some weeks into traumatized grief. Afterwards Jan and I wash dishes together. I talk about not writing for the first time since my "that widow" moment with Abbey. "It bothers me," I admit for first time.

Jan nods.

"I care and I don't care and I don't know how to write now."

Rambling words mingle with washing water. Syllables still difficult to string together. Brain's connecting powers needing a good flushing out. Jan stays silent. Not fixing anything. Hearing, the most important verb in the moment. Next morning enter empty office. Sit down. Make myself journal. "F----,f--,f-----,!"

Free association, random thoughts, raw emotions, lots of curse words. Crap all writers shovel through when abstracting emotions into words. Write each morning for about a week or two about nothing, everything, and maybe for the first time without an idea of what these strings of syllables can become.

Grief having no goal except pain eradication. Act of familiar ritualized discipline reopening small spring of words though. Reintegrating something internal. Slowly with the awkwardness of an adolescent. Begin looking forward to morning chore. Words coating pain with creative balm. Friend Jan says, "Pay attention."

"How?" I beg.

"God is disruptive," she replies.

"It will be healing," suggest my therapists. "Part of the journey."

Crap, I think. I hate this journey.

Blue Birthday

How to celebrate or mark Paul's fifteenth birthday? Spend hours in kitchen preparing favorite dishes the day before, on Sunday. Forming new Sabbath practice. Cooking on other days not happening. Not like when Tony was alive. This Sabbath making Swedish meatballs, mashed potatoes, ground beef stew, and lemon bars for Paul's requested birthday cake. Cooking connecting my children to me and our family including those who came before us.

For brief time feel seeds of something good. Me, mashing meat with eggs, milk, allspice, until mixture balls up. Paul and Ricky in and out of my way. Laughing. Telling jokes. Eyes bright with shared mischief. Together moving Tony's office furniture from garage into our daily lives. "I always have to back down the stairs," Paul says.

"Deal with it, Bud," Ricky replies.

Followed by shared commentary. Me, cringing at content. Sending them into pealed laughter. Accompanied by bangs, "oops," and "shit." Dents and scrapes appearing on walls. Small things, unimportant now.

Focus on our sons, problem-solving, working together, listening to each other. Receiving sparkles of pain relief off Tony's office furniture. Endorphins floating off inanimate objects. Left over from healing others in that space. Tony's words slipping off arm chairs into their hearts. "Do you want to feel better or do better?"

Understand Tony shares my pride this night. Exchange glances across steaming kitchen. Both amazed by lack of whining or push back. And again later, when Paul shovels driveway. Complaints absent or floating away on snow's crisp air. Tony murmuring, "Those are my boys!"

Our journey fraught with pain showing us once again little by little to be a family of joy and love. One without Tony here. But knowing he loves us still. "Please God," I pray dishing Sunday dinner up, "please help us rely on each other."

Paul wakes next day. Stomach in flames three months, three weeks, and two days into our pain-filled roller coaster. Adding physical pain to emotional. Punch doctor's numbers on phone. Push for appointment. Today. Tomorrow at very latest. Return to bed, exhausted. Tired of watching Paul and Ricky suffer. In trauma plus grief plus multiple mysterious, complicated health problems. Sighs this morning speaking to the brutality inflicted upon us. Contain silent prayers for good relief for Paul. My held-back tears, plaints for his life's rebuilding. Relief cannot come too soon. A true gift for this, his birthday.

Journal Entries

Three months, three weeks, five days.

Three choices. Keep pushing Paul to attend school, home school, or move to St. Paul, Minnesota, where I can attend seminary full-time. Maybe a fourth option: accept this year as bumpy for him. For me. He needs grieving space. My own needs in his way. Wanting rebuilding to begin now. Misunderstand this time as foundation. Enter Paul's sanctified, safe space. He doesn't look up from screen.

"Goodnight, Paul. I love you."

"Sure," he replies.

Crawl into bed. Hear Ricky leaving. Send him off with nightly lament. "I love you, Ricky. Be safe."

"Always am."

Heart pounding "bullshit, bullshit, bullshit."

"I love you too," he says entering the night.

Tony's death leaving me figuring everything out alone for our children. Thinking always of what Tony would say or do. Needing in some way to show him I'm taking care of our sons. Marit saying during therapy, "You will begin to parent without Tony."

Understand maybe I already do. Smile despite fears this night. Pray in night's quiet. "God, give me strength. Help me not burn out in this unasked-for journey. Circulate small shards of hope within my heart."

Almost four months.

Have I traded one extreme emotion for another? What is my role as a widow? What should I expect of myself in this role? I feel I must play act for others when all I really want to do is live my life. Which includes missing Tony, his voice, his laugh, his warm eyes, his people perceptions, his own brand of joie de vivre. But don't want to pretend I like our home torn up with The Men's Center stuff. Like the box of old electronics cords, ten years' worth, awaiting detangling and fate. Strewn across ping pong table. Lying dormant in grief. Surrounded by other boxes deemed important, such as tax returns and seven years' worth of receipts. Next to boxes of business cards too precious for tossing. All creating necessary tasks not feeding me.

More nourished yesterday during worship. Standing in front of assembled congregation. Publicly praying for those outside our walls. Not hijacked by grief for once if only for a few hours.

Think this day, maybe I am fragile and vulnerable. Or maybe I am strong and not the sum total of traumatic experience, grief, and loss. Maybe I am me in this specific situation living as God's child. Named and claimed here on earth. Tony living on elsewhere as God's beloved.

Widow Writer

January. Five months. Paul's school attendance sporadic. Haul myself to high school for school conferences. Stand in middle of cafeteria. People walking, sitting, and standing everywhere. Conversations buzzing around me. Can't figure out what to do next. Exhausted. See publisher of regional press. Lives up the street from us, toward the lake. Sat on a school committee together a few years ago. Follows my blog. Enjoys a good joke. Like when I said, "Steve, I'm going to 'accidently' drop a manuscript in your yard next time I walk the dog."

Steve moves through swirling crowd. Speaks of my first blog post since Tony died. The one about closing The Men's Center. Continuing a conversation we hadn't been having.

"Steve, will you publish my work?"

"If it's like that blog post, sure."

Paul not doing well in school. Go home bone-tired. Deflated by life. But with storms of syllables thundering in brain. Twisting into sentences. See Steve a few days later. Carrying an armload of manila envelopes into our small-town post office. "You opened a floodgate."

Not convinced this floodgate helps me.

"That was the point," he says. "I meant to."

"Are you really interested in something from me?"

"Yeh."

"I...I don't know. I don't. I don't know if I can do this."

"Why don't you send me a chapter? You can do that."

"Maybe."

Don't believe I can. Not so good at belief. Took years to believe Tony really loved me. In our beginnings often uttering, "Do you still love me?"

Tony, calm, factual, repetitive. "Still."

Later tables turning. During moments of ire at his behavior. Small smile playing on his lips. "Still?" he asked.

After church on Sunday, tell Abbey about possible book. Externally processing different thoughts wrapped in apprehension. Finally giving in. "Well I'm not having any sex so I might as well write the damn book!"

Abbey explodes, laughter gaining the attention of our friend Lori. "I think celibacy is a form of spirituality," she says.

"Maybe chosen celibacy is. Forced celibacy isn't," I say.

My hormones are old news to Abbey. Recent walks together include rants on injustices of full range of feelings from devastation, anger, betrayal, to missing intimacy with Tony. Given nature of Tony's death, naively assumed a year or two of automatic abstinence. New betrayal emerges out of haze. During sunny, warm afternoon eating lunch alfresco with Linnea and Tom. Waiter walking away from our table. My eyes following his derriere. Therapists celebrate yearning as life force erupting from my essence. Indication of desire to keep living. Beginning of shock's end in sudden grief and traumatic experience. I am not so sure. Still convinced such feelings should take a year or two off under the circumstances.

Friends elevating current situation. Pretending I adopt spiritual vow called celibacy. Putting a positive, philosophical spin on my yuck. Using energy force once put toward a mutual and intimate relationship into writing a book. Inherent complications of love, in all its beauty, fused into some form of work. Poured away from heart and into product. Except I profoundly grieve. Pushed daily to emotion's edge. Grief's abstinence not chosen kind nor celibacy. New friend Elaine, a widow, pastor, certified psycho-therapist, writer assures me over our first three-hour lunch, "This time will pass."

"When?" I ask.

Read through Tony's professional library on love. Under-stand that my experience is part of our pre-wired neurological systems. Wired for relationships, especially love relationships. Humans returning again and again to our first love attachments as infants—our parents or caregivers. As adults, either recreating early relationship of love or attempting to create emotionally responsive love we needed then through partner now.

Marit reminds me everything I experience now I feel in extreme intensity. Her analysis correct. Emotions ride waves. Despair returns after feeling sunshine's warmth. Rant at peo-ple, world, insurance agents, accountants, what happened to us. Then forget how to open a jar of tomato sauce.

And guilt? Guilt attaches to all emotions. Haunting me. In flashbacks, parenting, moments with friends, flashes of finding a man attractive, making future plans, living, writing. How can I possibly survive? Or keep the house up? Or parent? Or sleep night after night alone in our bed without Tony's warmth radi-ating my way. Without reassurance of waking him if sleep avoids me with worry and anxiety. Without the small sounds he made just living filling up quiet. Why isn't he here when I need him most?

Unexpected, unwelcomed yearnings reveal fear of living on alone. Living without Tony. New widow books warns me of this tendency with honesty and love. Relaying stories of women not really able to assess another's character in grief. Marrying people with high needs, addiction issues, or prone to anger, violence. Friend tells story of her father-in-law remarrying too quickly. Therapists say, "Be careful. Wait two years."

Lunch again with new friend Elaine. Assures me reeling emotions will subside. Stare in disbelief. "How can any of my feelings leave?" I ask. "Or the body pains grief brings on? Or my mind's inabilities to think, plan, and function? Or my eating aversion, the ever-present knot in my stomach taking up all the space normally reserved for nourishment? Or the pervasive fatigue wreaking havoc in my body? Or these waves of agitation shaking my limbs and heart and running wild when trying to rest?"

As months progress, Elaine's words reveal truth. When a friend lovingly suggests I could begin practice dating, I am appalled. When other friends admire my dress asking how many men asked me out that day, my body retracts. Understanding that what began last September constitutes the continued search for one I lost. Yearning for him who knew me. Saw me for me. Went beyond mere noticing my tone of voice, dress, way I wear my hair. Twenty-three years ago diving in. Laughing with me, holding my hand, making plans with me, hearing my pain, sharing my joy.

Early days of grief and trauma manic, compulsive. Bad choices in money, work, or love easily accomplished. If getting rid of too much of Tony's professional library was the worst decision made during this time, then in newfound wisdom I am lucky, blessed, both. Blessed by people both reining me in and pushing me forward. Giving warnings as gifts. Laughing at hormones as compassion. Nudging me to write as saving grace.

Soul Singing

Bought at an art fair years ago on the banks of the Mississippi River, the linoleum print hangs in our living room. Hues of black, navy, and night sky blue set against cream with streaks of orange. Like sunset over the horizon here in the Midwest. Except vertical. Emanating from figure of a silhouetted, curvaceous woman. Arms rising toward heavens as if in blessing while glowing circular mass rotates in her upper body. Erupting out. First as vapor. Then into stars and doves. Soaring into heavens as if coming directly from her very essence. Caption reading, "my soul sings."[8]

We bought the painting in celebration of my self-discovery of hearing words and music dancing in my head at odd moments of each day. Thirty-eight and postpartum after birth of our second son, I heard an organ introit. Not some composer's work but mine. In my head while showering. Escaping intense needs of our newborn babe and young son. Told Tony still damp from brief respite, "I'm either having a psychotic break or a brain tumor."

Mental health professional I married replied, "You're just being Swedish."

Not amused at all by his commentary. In days following, heard stories in my head as well. Began writing soon after. Amidst diapers, dinner, and during naps. Most days wanting every word just right. Learning flow through trial and error. Having small successes. Manuscripts mounting in office. Sad, no, agitated when no time to write.

After being accepted into seminary just a few weeks before Tony died, I wondered how to write while training for my new vocation. Talked together of my sadness. Tony trusting my abilities. "You'll figure it out."

Writing now. In bed. Hiding. When I wake, before sleeping, often in spare moment or two during day. Nightstand accumulating all necessary writing tools: paper scraps, notepads, journals, pens, pencils, a chocolate bar or two. Dark. European. Less wax. Story spilling out onto pages of Tony's journal. One I gave him years ago when setting sail toward his own dream. My words mixing in with his. Because I cannot mix with him now.

Some days words erupting with speed and force. Fingers flying accelerando through notes connecting thought to thought in quick succession. Pen and paper not quick enough to suffice flow

---

[8] Artist, Lori Biwer Stewart.

of emotions turned words. Turn to Tony's laptop. One bearing reminders of what was and is not now. Other days words resist. Eat too much chocolate. Drink too much tea. Pummel myself as caffeine feels like trauma's adrenaline and cortisol's inner shakings. Both chemicals I want eradicated from my body.

On good days, fuss with words on paper. Adding here, subtracting there. Shaping. Breathing. Walking away. Eating more chocolate. Letting words sit. Incorporate until whole takes on shape. Not unlike moment when separate ingredients form cohesive ball. Assuring me the meatloaf will once again be ready for dinner. And somehow everything will be alright.

My fractured soul, still singing. Profound sadness and sorrow emanating from molecular level. Coursing through veins. Lamenting like the psalmist. Canting like our print.

Questioned Opportunity

Pounding heart. Clenching stomach. Gagging throat. Flashing back external. Not mine. Paul in tears. Describing beach in aftermath. He, feeling alone. Me at hastily set-up ground zero. Frozen to ground. Shut down in self-protection. Collapsing inward. Becoming one of Tony's sayings. "The person at ground zero goes into the bunker."

Paul left outside bunker. Ricky kayaking downriver. Searching for Tony. People rushing toward river's banks. Gawking. Asking, "What happened?"

A man tells Paul, "You did exactly the right thing. Breaking the current."

A woman calls Tony stupid. To Paul's face. After he asks group to call 911 for a man in trouble.

My beloved son, mostly alone. Because I am unable to bring him into my arms. Reassure him. Love him. Listening, five months and one week later. Sitting at one end of green family room sofa. Paul stretched out. Allowing me only to rub his calves with gentle hands while my internal desperation rises. Breathe instead, avoiding explanations of my actions in midst of unimaginable terror and shock on the day I froze.

Try to listen. Bat away internal thoughts. How many sessions of talk therapy and Eye Movement Desensitization Recovery (EMDR)[9] and somatic movement therapy[10] will it take? How many to rewire my brain from that day? How many times must I rewrite the narrative? Eradicating guilt? My inability to help and save Tony? My inability to parent my children?

First flashback occurred that night. On ride home in dark of night. Tony's head going under river's water. Replayed. Rewound. Replayed. Rewound. Replayed. Mind forcing me to relive. Live again. Again. Brain glitching. Spinning like tires in mud. Needing push out. Flash followed by words: I forgive myself. Forgiveness stilling flash. Only for a second. Flash, forgiveness, flash, forgiveness. Like a mantra in the night. Shaking, voice pitched high, share flashback forgiveness tool with our sons next day. In fanatical attempt to parent. "If you see the scene in your mind, just say "I forgive myself."

Ricky and Paul's faces betraying their thoughts, who is this woman?

Their mother lost at beach. Replaced by shrinking woman sitting where their mother used to work. Staring where their mother used to think. Sighing where their mother used to sing. Crying where their mother used to speak. A stranger inhabit-

---

[9] "EMDR (Eye Movement Desensitization and Reprocessing) is a psychotherapy that enables people to heal from the symptoms and emotional distress that are the result of disturbing life experiences." "Eye Movement Desensitization and Reprocessing," EMDR Institute, Inc, accessed March 3, 2021, https://www.emdr.com/what-is-emdr/.

[10] Somatic Movement Therapists "use knowledge of anatomy with combinations of movement, sound, breath, touch and imagery to deepen their clients' understanding of themselves in movement. Somatic Movement Practitioners work with the body but acknowledge that movement affects the dimensions of psyche and spirit as well." "About ISMETA," ISMETA, accessed March 14, 2020, https://ismeta.org/about-ismeta.

ing our home. Wandering presence unwelcomed. "I hate you," Paul tells this stranger. Strong emotion ordering her out of his space.

Therapy asks this stranger to disappear. Take guilt with them. Leave me in charge, mending wounds infected with emotional trauma's bacterium. Ripping insides apart again and again. Traumatic, complex grief sounding alarm in soul but for what? How did we get here?

Stitches break today. Paul's. Mine. Shifting day's plans. No school again today for Paul. I reschedule meetings, cancel appointments. Schedule's security obliterated by grief and trauma demands. Paul sleeps, weary from our interchange. I bake apple torte and pie. Make phone calls. To Ricky's college savings plan. "How do I change the plan's successor?"

To his college financial aid office. "We've had a change in income due to death."

To the Federal Financial Aid office only to be told, "Be sure to mark the marital status form box with widow."

God, please let me out of this death mess. Receive no reply. Ask another question. How do loving, smart, well-educated people end up here, dragging their children with them? Again, no answer.

Drive Paul downtown for therapy later this same day. Angst growing with each mile. Into anger bursting through body. Internal containers overflowing. Gushing out into full-blown anxiety attack. Wishing I still drank or smoked or even embraced casual sex. Anything to take the edge off this day. Last anxiety attack over a month ago, around Christmas. Anticipated during holidays. Was prepared for it. Like an expected yet unwanted guest. This one, a surprise.

Leave Paul at therapist's office. Need air. Walk out onto cobbled street. Words whirling in brain. Waiting to be written down on scraps of paper. Adding new knowledge about Paul at the beach. Now haunting me on errand. Taking me past Tony's old office. Adrenaline popping through arms. Remembering Albert Einstein quote found on magnet in Tony's office. "In the middle of difficulty lies opportunity."

In the middle of my difficulty lie words documenting my most personal self. What would Einstein think? Tony? My children? What do I think? Complete errand. Sit in therapist's reception area. Legs crossed. Hands clasped in lap. Body small. Tight fortress. Protecting heart from world.

Home. Cook full meal. Serve shepherd's pie, kale chips, apple pie made earlier. Say to air, "I guess you won't be home for dinner."

Tony not home for dinner tonight. Or yesterday. Or the day before that. Never home again. Leaving empty place at table, in hearts. Garage door silent. No purr at dinner time signaling arrival home. For dinner. To us. Even for one last time. Think through tears, "Hey Einstein, where's the opportunity here?"

Journal Entry

Five months, one week.

Asked my mother the first week, "How many death certificates do I need?"

"Fifteen," she replies.

For months stuffing envelopes with federal blue, embossed documents. To every business or organization needing proof. Avoiding cause of death line. The one reading, "drowning."

Balanced Breath

"The body's midline is in front of us. Not in us as most people think. But in front of us," Meg, my somatic movement therapist, says holding me upright. As we both look in her mirror.

Meg stands me on my own. Lets go of me. Says, "That's how we balance, by seeing our midline out there, in front of us."

Waiver. Meg catches me. Again. As she has many times during trauma recovery. Today teaching me to catch myself. By focusing on my balance and freeing the clumped up mass of muscles along my lower left spine. A hardened compaction causing me pain since early in the summer before Tony died. Meg's wisdom discovering all my body's small and large traumas through her fingers. Her healing hands learning deep truths about me through what my muscles share with her. "Did you ever wear a back brace?" she asks one day early in our work together.

"A Milwaukee brace," I tell her, "From age thirteen to sixteen."

Old Milwaukee brace of my childhood, big and bulky. Contraption used to curb leanings of overly curvaceous spine otherwise known as scoliosis. Metal bars beginning at neck. One in front and two in back ending where my bottom met my upper thighs. Around my torso a girdle of hardened plastic strapping me in. Smelling of sweat. Compliant in wearing it. For twenty-three and one-half hours per day for almost three years. Released gradually. Once fully free placed brace out with garbage one day. Erasing its meaning. Or so I thought. Hauntings beginning in college with a series of back pains. Weakened muscles striving to work once more. Atrophying for three years. Various forms of bodywork, physical therapy, and Alexander Technique help. Soon after college, an X-ray of my left jaw reveals the pillowed disk between jaw joint, squashed like an old woman's. Pain both physically real and emotionally silent as dreams of singing professionally wane.

Need to know why disk is flat? Perhaps connected to scoliosis? Doctors, orthodontists, and dentists disagree with me. Find medical library in New York City where I live. Paw through mounds of paper research articles among dust, quiet, and others seeking answers. One day finding article about Milwaukee brace's impact on wearer's body. Neckpiece causing jaw problems over time. Medical team and I both right. They understood scoliosis was not the problem. I made the connection. Treatment, the culprit.

Leave singing. Leave New York City. Begin anew in Chicago. Study and obtain a master's degree in early childhood development. Meet Tony. Fall in love. Create a life together. Three moves, one house, two babies, and ten years later study voice again. Connect pushing sensation on larynx to front of brace's neckpiece. Realization shifts my singing toward what I always thought I could do.

Thinking then my history with the Milwaukee brace complete. Wrapped up nicely in healing through all the years of body work, research, and connections. Ongoing efforts keeping body's betrayal at bay. Surprised to discover in wake of Tony's death that the brace still haunts my muscles. Body "working off old data," as Tony would say.

Meg reshaping my fascia, the thin sack of tissue enclosing muscles. Week after week mending all my body's wounds. "Give me a big yawn," she demands. "Now another one."

Complying once again with experts' orders. Following directions into my girlhood body before brace. Delighting in movement. Feeling free. Shedding brace's muscle memory. Brace's death only death I now rejoice in.

Released from physical hurting, strong will to live emerges in this new balancing act called life without Tony. Breath still frozen, shallow. Full balance needing breath. My therapeutic duo, Meg and Marit push me. "Breathe," they calmly command. "Deep breath. Fill up your lungs. Fill up your stomach."

Marit makes observations. "You are strong."

"I don't believe you."

Meg adds midline words, information. "People with scoliosis cannot balance from within. The curve upsets the mind's thought line trying to run up and down the spine."

Healers combined mantras construct internalized reminders to inhale oxygen, breathe out carbon dioxide. Breath beginning outside of me moving both in and out. Midline staying ahead. Out there in front of me. Where life lives in this world, in the lives of others. Breath and balance not allowing death to supersede life.

Untethered

From first evening standing on deck of rented farmhouse. Hands shaking. Throat clogging. Trying to get cell phone reception. Voices weaving in and out. Earlier at the beach, not letting go of ground. Remain unleashed months into trauma's reactions. Unbounded, cordless, ungrounded, floating, untethered. Want to run away to Greece. Avoid business bills. Fill our bed with pillows, books, chocolate, and Tony's laptop. Find a savior, a handsome one. Scream at walls. Just drive around or away. Use my credit card.

Resist Greece and finding a savior. Plan trip to Europe under flimsy guise of visiting family. But really just want to leave. Escape this constant whatever this is. Fling it off into an abyss. Be free of these feelings for a few hours and without numbing out. But need ways to stay here in this place we call home. Of course, children help. Even if one now lives across town in a brown apartment with smelly hallways. Eating sale pork chops for days. Foraging for food when home. Often finding none.

Therapy, too, keeps me home. Hard to find a good therapist let alone the four we require. Week punctuated by these sessions as well as church, meetings, paperwork, and Paul's schedule. Everything else needing to be done, accomplished in bed assisted by Tony's computer. Often in few hours each morning when world is quiet. Keeping company with tea, dark chocolate, emotions painted on paper. Time of predictable solace. Evenings crawling back into bed. Flattened by day. Especially if some happening put me under. Like going out for a social event. Looking forward to it for days. While there, wanting to escape back home, to safety, to our bed.

Each morning rise, out of necessity. Feet sweaty in slipper socks. Pad across living room to Paul's bedroom. Wake Paul lost in sleep. Attempt breakfast. Abort meal and school. Next, straighten hair. Curly and long in grief. As if my genetic, hormonal structure changed. Rummage for makeup. Lengthen lashes, dust eye lids, powder nose. Move to closet. Slip on another new dress. Crawl back into bed. Back to words moving through head. Strung into lines of print. Not stalling as spoken words do in grief and trauma's recovery. But out through fingers. Telling all I cannot say to the world. What others do not want to hear. Writing as refusal. A rebellious act, not holding pain's truth for others. Sparing them sorrow's reality.

Take solace. In our bed each morning. Working through word swirls. Uncover emotions and memories once dormant. Dive into depths finding truths as treasures whether they be beautiful or painful. Not believing I didn't see or couldn't comprehend necessity of writing in beginning. Output growing, if not toward sun then just out into world. Sputtering forward from soul. Giving me something on which to hang my heavy heart. Tracking this time so different from other times. Documenting some elemental truths, mine. Others.

Or maybe writing just keeps me in bed. One we shared in love, with children, dog, books, mouth guards, CPAP machine, neck pillows, eyeglasses, tissues, words of love, words of frustration, sleeplessness, snoring, and daily mumbled I love you near morning. And that's it. Writing may be many things to me now. But this morning ritual keeps me closest to our coupleship, a word you, my love, used in your work. Even with your books now gone from your nightstand and the CPAP machine you hated from underneath the bed and the myriad of charging cords populating your side of things and the stray sock or tissue tucked into the bedclothes. Your smell, too, erased from the sheets along with the warmth of your body no longer lingering as if you rose early to read on the couch downstairs.

But our bed is here. Each morning and again each evening planting myself against propped pillows. Covering my legs with our comforter and quilt. Staying planted for our children. For my own dreams. For what is left of the us, we became and no longer are. Crying. Making no sense out of what happened. Wondering when my next therapy session is. Thinking I should call a friend. Saying no. Not really wanting to share our intimacy. Guarding us for fear the last wisps of what is left will also soon be gone.

Remembering as I hide under feathers warming my cold feet (which you complained of each winter) your cells coursed through my body. Weaving in and out of mine as I grew our children in my womb. You will never fully leave any part of me even when I eventually choose to leave our bed. Maybe this scares me, this thought of always being tethered to you. Bringing you along just as my attachment to my parents never leaves. But now there are three of you riding with me in life. All loves, ghosts in my heart two of you with one still smiling at me over the phone thankfully. Adding in our sons, I walk not alone but with a caravan of souls entwined with mine. Laced together by love's connections. Hearing the first line of that old hymn "Blessed be the Ties that Bind" in my head over and over again. Revisiting the last stanza realizing how much my ancestors understood loss and grief. "But we shall still be joined in heart..."

Secure right now under our duvet printed with bold leaves in greens and blues. Its weight keeping me centered. Reminding me to stay connected in love here and now. Which is different from being connected to the ground or to the memory of our love. Living our love, even in your absence, through loving the living anchors me. Propels me into each day, minute by minute becoming future. Love continuing. Launched from a strong dwelling place of safety. Rapprochement's home from forays into an unknown world post-you. A world where even a high school band concert causes heart to beat too fast. Breath to catch in throat. Head bend into paper program. Avoiding other's gaze while waiting to return later to this place, our bed.

Knowing each day as I awake and each night as I escape into paper or word or sleep that we were good if only because we loved as verb, commitment, way of life. And because we were good, I will be good in time and our children will be good as well. And what I truly long for, along with your smile, ready laugh, vocational commitment, and earthly love of the boys and me, is our elemental connection spoken each time our eyes met across the room. And when in our bed our hands touched at dawn.

Family Still

Shields up. Swords out. In response to some well-meaning person stuck in cluelessness shaking her head. Her internal thoughts spilling out. Past my personal boundary. "Your family is ripped apart!"

"We are still family!"

On my watch, I insist we are family to each other regardless of what happened. Demand others see or pretend to see us the same way.

Wishful Litany

I wish you were here to see Paul's shoulders broaden out and his limbs shoot long and his brain go click, click, click when excited. Or watch his first tentative accelerations in the school parking lot one very snowy day. Or laugh at our talks about sex that, really, I would rather have left up to you. Or witness his courage and humor in facing his own medical mystery with patience and fortitude, doctor after doctor. Or how he cues me about his grief. Mostly though I wish you were here to jump up and down together on the trampoline. You, laughing the whole time. Fatherhood's joys spilling out. Filling up the back yard. I wish you were here.

I wish you were here to embrace the leaving of Lyme disease from Ricky's body. See his eyes brighten, his focus return. His body heal and grow into a man's physique and his hair look golden like you always wanted in our children. Even though his is the color of chestnuts glowing with good health. And hear about his first college paper or test. Viewing from afar or in your mind's eye as he visits your parents and my mother on his own. And see him play music once again. Smiling and clapping like you once did after ordering a pretend drink at the bar because he asked you to blend in a bit with the other men. Mostly though to embrace him becoming himself again after all those years of chaos when Lyme affected his behavior but none of us knew it. I wish you were here.

I wish you were here holding my hand and I yours. Walking on Sunday afternoons, moisture spitting on us from low-lying Midwestern clouds. Your palm thick, padded. Mine boney, small. Having a walk and talk as you called our hikes. Mending through simple touch and shared steps what we put on hold when our children were so ill. Each handheld step saying silently, "It has been good and is good and will continue to be good."

Friends driving by, waving. Later saying, "I saw you two out for one of your meetings."

I wish you were here. Sharing your work with me at dinner. Your calling filled with hopes for the future, frustrations, accomplishments, and your next book. Vocation intermingling with your overflowing pride in our boys. Then after dinner taking me in your arms. Dancing in our kitchen as dishes crust over and sauces solidify. Wearing that "I am a contented man smile," of yours. I wish you were here.

Seeing all the trees and bushes we planted during the drought years. In their maturing beauty framing our yard in natural sanctuary. Sitting together. Watching night breezes, or a hummingbird, or the moon. Remembering all the grumblings and sweat now rewarded in shade, flowers, and the singular beauty a mere tree brings to the world. Smiling at our wasted negativity. Cursing hardened clay when creation's wise worth asks so little of us. I wish you were here.

Hearing my rocky first sermon. Accompanying me on my crazy call to ministry. When feeling low, placing your hand gently between my shoulder blades. Assuring me we travel together on this journey. Once again jumping into the unknown universe like we did with The Men's Center. Only God's spirit guiding us. I wish you were here.

Seeing the small stuff like my hair grow long. Which you wished to see once again in your lifetime. Laughing lovingly at the highlights covering strands of grey. Expressing amazement how laundry stays in dryer for days now. Kitchen looks disheveled. Wardrobe grows dress by dress. Delighting in the care I take of myself for once. I wish you were here.

Basking in all we built: a marriage, children, a business, vocations, an extended circle of family and friends, a home. A place to begin each day anew. Awash with another chance to love and love better. A place to face the difficult emotional work of life. Love always living here. A working sanctuary. Home existing between each of us and in our hearts. Here with us now. Balancing our current reality toward healing instead of pain. "Tony, I miss you not here."

"Jen, that's your humanity."

Survival Practice

Collecting Noises: In your journal list all the sounds of your beloveds. Sighs, coughs, throat clearing, snores, moans, and laugh. Collect these moments. Touch each one with a finger kiss.

Prayer

God of aching hearts, lift pain from inner depths. Hold pain with love. Lead pain into life. Amen.

Christmas dinner 2011 in Des Plaines, Illinois.

Making Norwegian lefse with my mother.

Goofing off with Uncle Peter.

IV. Spring Thaw

"Don't forget your tool box."
—Tony Rodriguez

Blessing

Head bent. Eyes closed. Chest constricting. Reaching for breath. Words floating over me, into the congregation. Hands on me. Belonging to people saying "yes" to God's call for me into ministry. Hands turning me. Away from ordained and rostered. Toward people in pews. Friends, strangers, acquaintances, family. Gathered here to worship this Sunday. Service including blessing. On beginning seminary. Tomorrow. First class, first day. See tear-filled eyes looking at me. Matching mine. Joining in journey. Tears, my true blessing from God.

Aching Arms

Still crying in store aisles at seven months. Mostly in snack aisle. Tony wasn't a cracker snack guy. He was sweet, not salty. Yet the wide aisle stuffed with puffy bags of salt, fat, and starch becomes my normal place for tearful eruptions. Between bags of pretzels and whole grain crackers. For reasons unknown to me. Maybe I just find snack culture depressing. Like my grief. Maybe I find the two hundred choices overwhelming. Like my grief. Maybe the two towering sets of shelves overloaded with overstimulating packaging feels imprisoning. Like my grief.

Tears flare each trip three-quarters into shopping list. Almost at the end of each necessary, public outing. Only baking aisle and fresh vegetables to go. Home's safety tantalizingly near. Dangling like a carrot on a string. Weary to shed public protective emotional armor. Checkout lane offering two stands of last-chance goodies. Framing me like a fortress during wait for the checkout women I prefer. Older eyes assessing my untold story.

But trauma reactions mixed with grief thrive on unpredictability. Tears flow today on other side of immense store. In auto parts aisle. Searching for replacement bulbs for car headlights. Headlights burning out every month since Tony died. Ricky offering to swap burned-out ones for new. Not quite trusting that the Lyme disease is gone enough for Ricky to do so. But his idea to do it ourselves saves us money and me time in hauling car over to Tony's trusted mechanic across town. Tony choosing mechanic closer to work than home. Making sense at the time.

Hunch over the cart avoiding choices. Lower arms aching again. Adrenaline coming out of hiding after a few dormant months or maybe just weeks. Allowing reprieve of sorts. Neurotransmitters of trauma's pain hiding. Contributing to illusion of being healed. Physical and emotional pain vacating my body in increments. Human rebuilding process both internal and external laying foundation in muscles, tendons, joints, bones, and organs. Healing filling arms with something else. Something healthy.

But in this aisle remember all that my aching arms represent. Our chaos, sudden loss. Bearings uprooted. Drifting along and away. Leaving focus for only this intimate experience called grief with added trauma cocktail. All infused in my arms. Locked in. Shooting. Aching. Tingling. Arms telling truth. Arms aching to "let the scream out," as Tony would say. Internal pain, a form of stunted or imprisoned screams. Each unheard wail, a prickle, pulse, and ping of pain. Stuck within. No door out. Carrying grief like loaded grocery bags. Weight in arms as heart sinks lower.

Filling up every molecule of my being grief's pain never solely in heart, arms, and tears. External sphere, the only place lacking truth. Outside body world swirls around. Others' denial of their own physical pain stemming from grief and trauma. Distancing themselves in unconscious recognition.

Today tears flow. Among strangers. Showing world all I left undone in my marriage to Tony. All the love cut off abruptly. Violently. My arms holding emotion's complexities instead of Tony. Telling me stories of our life together and our life torn apart. "Oh, God," my tears wail. "Oh, God."

Spring Break

We are not where we normally spend this week. Moving us from point A (home) to point B (Arizona) is a lost skill set. In another month Paul travels to Florida with the high school marching band. Ricky went last October to visit friend, sometimes girl-friend, Emily in Tampa. I've been to Minneapolis three times since Tony died.

Traveling right now, if I think straight for thirty seconds, not affordable. But I am sad staying home. Deeply sad. My body hurts all over with a dull, throbbing ache. Accompanied by internal twitching in my arms, legs, and buttocks. Body remembering other spring breaks. This remembering called an anniversary issue. Because for most of our married life we vacationed right about now. Tony and our sons sitting three in a row on flight to Mesa. Me across the aisle basking in a magazine or talking with complete stranger sitting next to me. Only to be tapped on the shoulder. "What kind of snacks did you bring?"

Once settled at my mother's winter quarters, swimming. Making runs for burgers and fries. Organizing hikes no one under the age of twenty wanted to go on. Basking in day's heat while checking weather at home. Watching hummingbirds buzz. Catching glimpses of javelina babies following their mothers through prickly brush. Relaxing together or in parallel. Weaving in and out of conversations, card games, tourist activities. Needed moments of reconnecting and restoring. Small relational cuts and wounds healing thanks to slower days and nature.

This spring break in Iowa City. Smelling of melting snow and earth ready for reawakening. Light brightening each day and lingering longer at night. On empty university campus today. Three of us lunching at local diner after reapplying for passports. In passport office Ricky and Paul posing for new photos stone faced. Cracking up each other and the passport officer. More merriment at diner's table waiting for food. Private jokes flying between them reminiscent of another time. Boy banter returning for a few minutes giving us all a slice of hope. Maybe a glimpse at future.

Back home feel anxious again. Unsettled, overwhelmed, and uncentered. Feeling stress creep up through calves aiming for vulnerabilities in neck, arms, stomach. Bearing weight of upcoming midterms in first semester of seminary. Followed by another interview with synod candidacy committee and revisions of an article on sudden grief. Spring break no break from life's demands, trauma's aftereffects, and grief's ongoing pain. Maybe it's the book I'm reading. Maybe the change in schedule. Maybe grief lingers on. Waiting for its own kind of spring. Asking us to "stay in this space," as Tony said. Stay in this space of sorrow mixed with healing. Old data "making new data," another one of Tony's sayings, through trauma recovery therapy and living. Writing our story of what was, is, and can be. Mostly though, I just miss Tony during our first spring break without him.

Knowing

Hands move through motions of making a meal. Breathing a bit while chopping vegetables. Look up from cutting board to outside world. My thinking mind blanks as my heart bursts.

"We are okay. Or enough okay for now. Or better than we've been." my heart says after seven months.

Maybe for first time in trauma. In grief, I know. Recognize something good after all the crap. Goodness creating tears. Dropping on counter. Not in grief. In something bigger. Quiet joy mixing with sounds of sons in other parts of our home. Dropping toilet lids and banging doors.

"Hey, flush the toilet!"

"Pick up your stinkin' underwear."

Sounds of living weaving into day's reflections. Born from observable data collected point by point in our journey since Tony's death. Ricky in college, part-time. One year ago, he sat on family room sofa. Playing video games for hours. Painting pictures on walls of storage room. Ropes tied into nooses, pistols, grim reaper. Lyme disease inflaming his brain. Friend's suicide inflaming his heart. Seeking solace in therapy, new diets, new doctors, and substances. But today he seems clearer. Calmer. Able to plan ahead. Study some. German, of all languages. My oldest son not well. But better. As if waking up from a bad dream. Asking, "What's for dinner?" Telling me, "Guten Abend, Mutter."

Paul talks again. Rehiring me as his parent, after firing me shortly after Tony died in my ongoing helplessness. Now taking refuge in what we jokingly call his "office." A space housed in the guest bedroom. Full of computer parts, a drone, antique furniture he hates, and his ever-present teenage smell. Tinkering. Waiting for skies to clear so he can fly the drone. Emerging from his den seeking food. "Dinner?" he asks.

Wanting his mother who cooks back. Finding her still struggling with putting ingredients together. Some days shards of bright light shine in his face regardless of my lost culinary skills.

"Can you make me some lemon bars?"

"Yes," I answer. Paul later eating all of my lopsided, slightly burned attempt.

Seminary studies combine with occasional freelance work for me. Part-time of course. Our reentry into daily life done in small increments. Time skewed by trauma. Powered down into slow motion. Accelerator pedal dismantled. In shop for repairs. No pickup date written on grief's calendar.

In seminary, I choose to learn biblical Hebrew. Parsing foreign verbs each day. Memorizing common nouns. Pretending participation during online classes. Looking the part. Faking it for my own heart's safety. Wondering why my brain on trauma and grief thought studying a foreign language would be a good idea. Misunderstanding my current limitations. Another cognitive distortion in trauma's afterlife.

Our collective healing progresses. Not evenly or predictably or consistently. Grief and trauma bucking linear movement and logical thinking. Yet standing in middle of kitchen today every cell in my body tells me something new. Speaks to me as revelation. As knowing. As gift. As recipient, giver, and receiver of hope.

Paul shunned hope's possibility. Ricky in illness could not care. I stood firm in hope's possibility. Found in one sentence in a book from Tony's library. Peter A. Levine writing, "Trauma doesn't have to be a life sentence."[11]

Highlighting these words and others like it as I read Tony's professional library instead of seminary books. Holding this sentence close. As prayer, mantra. Forging ahead in life partially out of necessity. Work providing solace. Routine giving me reason. Rebuilding, a mission. But behaviors, external. Following directives from pastors, therapists, family, and friends. In distress and emotional fatigue, I do just as I am told. Like the obedient child I once was. Pastor Peter telling me, "Give all your concerns to God each night."

Name them one by one silently before the universe. Force each one into something bigger through pushing palms. Followed by telling body, "Time to sleep." Because Meg told me to do so. Too overcome and overwhelmed by each day to argue with her seemingly simple suggestion. Finding my body feels the same way as my heart and mind.

---

[11] Peter A. Levine, *Healing Trauma: A Pioneering Program for Restoring the Wisdom of Your Body* (Boulder, CO: Sounds True, 2008), 3.

People speak of my courage, but really I am only following directions. Giving over my decisions to experts in new arena of trauma recovery and grief. Doing work of healing, yes. But living inside trauma and grief sucks. It is physically and emotionally painful. And all bodies work to escape pain. Mine included. But by following experts, I hope beyond hope to avoid escaping this hell through alcohol, numbing substances, sex, work, food, or any other way of covering up my pain (except dark chocolate). Which is to say, I know I am capable of doing so.

Today warmth and light filter in kitchen's sliding door. Releasing muscles frozen for months. Allowing a welling up. Not of wails and shaking shoulders. Tears today something of a smile. Upturned lips guiding future. "A lamp for my feet," as the psalmist says.[12]

Grief Displayed

"How are you doing? How are the boys?"

"Jennifer, I just heard. I am so sorry. How horrible for you."

"I know just what you are going through."

"Horrid. Simply horrid."

"How's seminary? When will you be done?"

There are some things about trauma recovery and grief I prefer keeping private. But early on I figure out the near impossibility of my desire. Still want it, this sense of invisibility at times. Space, too. An unseen circle surrounding me at about arm's length. A moat around emotional castle wall. Lines I want no one and no words to cross. Walls deflecting questions, comments. In the first months, my therapist Marit created a standard comeback line to all questions. Words rehearsed in her office until flowing easily from my mouth, creating a protective membrane for heart: "We miss Tony very much. But we were and are a resilient family."

---

[12] Psalm 119:105 (NRSV).

My appearance is deceiving. Even though I am frightfully thin and gaunt, others forget how deep wounds cut. Mourning ritual includes mending stitches torn away by the previous day. What hurts most is how others cease talking about Tony. Which includes Ricky, Paul, and I dancing around his absence at home. But we are the ones trying to figure out how to talk about him now. Me, focusing on his work. Paul just wanting to talk about his dad. Ricky, maybe a little of both.

Others act as if life fills in gaping hole left in our universe. Concealing Tony's life under an expensive granite stone up the street in city's cemetery. What I wouldn't give to hear from others, "You must miss Tony so very much."

Eight months of missing Tony. The process of becoming a pastor breaks open my few remaining crumbs of privacy. Creating vulnerability. Wondering whom to trust with my broken heart. Pastors, current and future, aren't always very good at complex grief laced with emotional trauma. Many just stare dumbfounded. Fumbling for words. "I don't know what to say."

"Well, you'd better figure this one out. The world is full of people like me."

Walk with torn open vulnerability. As if I'm recovering from heart surgery and the surgeon forgot to sew me back up, leaving internal organs and soul visible to all. No protective layers of skin and muscle encapsulating me. Making me now susceptible to others' shaming. Over lunch one day a pastor friend says, "You come off as a know-it-all."

Large, heaving sobs shake loose. Waiter fusses with our already filled water glasses. Friend's body shifts. "People say cruel things to pastors. I'm trying to prepare you."

"I think I've had enough cruelty for one year," I say.

Leaving home leaves me wide open for these overt and covert shaming acts delivered by well-meaning others. People playing therapist or expert. Whose words betray their own emotional pains, lack of expertise, and inability to feel what I feel. Adding instead more detonations to my emotional minefield. "Do you want to teach the class?" an adjunct instructor asks me during a seminary-required personal boundaries workshop. Her words meant to silence my expertise.

"Yes," I think. But instead say, "I'm not taking anything on right now since my husband died suddenly last August."

Her posture changes. Showing me she understands the line she crossed. My words once again giving notice to those whose own personal boundaries need work. "I'm so sorry," she says.

"Right," I think.

Comments on seminary papers go unread. Can't trust my reading ability. Tracking written words confuses my brain. Neural connecting highway undergoing reconstruction. Traffic slowed to one narrow lane each way, causing me to misread class times and term paper instructions.

Work with an editor new to me. Knows enough of my story to use care with her words. Sends thoughtful, quiet emails so as to not upset me with her editorial commentary and rewrite requests. Despite her compassion, writing article on sudden grief feels like being stuck in a bog slogging about. Similar to feelings of power-lessness. In the water. The day Tony slipped away from us.[13]

Not surprising who I rely on—therapists, other writers, editors. People able to withstand my pain. Keeping their own needs quiet. Never asking me to endure their suffering on top of my own. After a couple of months in seminary, my small group leader, Claire, asks to call me. Odd, I think. Arrange a time. Sprawl diagonally across bed. Hoping bed protects me from call's content. "I have no business being your precept leader," she says.

What does she mean?

Claire, like Aunt Linda, joins my shouts of "grief is normal" and "trauma recovery is possible!"

[13] Jennifer Ohman-Rodriguez. "Grief With No Warning," *Living Lutheran*, May 15, 2017. https://www.livinglutheran.org/2017/05/grief-with-no-warning/

While supporting my call to ministry. "You will be a wonderful pastor," she says.

Lasting Gifts

Here. Somewhere. Searched for since death. Named when found. Not like when life expects death. Those gifts, conscious. Tony's gifts scattered like puzzle pieces throughout our daily lives. Some gifts found in his litany of sayings.

"Everyone is annoying sometimes."

"That's goodness."

"Do you want to feel better or do better?"

"That's your humanity."

"Write a new narrative."

"How's that working for you?"

"That sounds like whoo, whoo to me."

"Are you guessing?"

Client sends package first week containing photo cards. Cards displaying Tony's sayings. Ones remembered in her own shock and grief. Some new to me. Others recognizable. Words from quiet man. Tony eating dinner with us. Listening to our banter. Head tilted toward plate. Piping up occasionally with one of his many sayings. Not really talking until boys off to own endeavors. Their food gulped in minutes. Leaving us in youth's wake. With plates half-full of cooling food. Launching into our work days. Sharing small successes, irritations. Tony often saying, "A client really got it today!"

Replying, "That's great." Thinking also, "Why wouldn't they? You are so good at what you do!"

Left alone now at table. Staring out sliding glass door. Looking into branches of large farm tree at yard's edge. Multiple stems housing birds and squirrels. Life scampering on limbs.

Last fall at The Men's Center, I combed through all of Tony's things. Looking for this man we love and lost. Still breathing somewhere in this space. Find him within pages of knowledge he held so dear. Information we now need. Paul pretending not to care. Ricky pulling a few books from piles destined for other places. Mostly ones on sex. Me, keeping books on trauma, addiction, the brain, teenagers, and relationships. Lugged home in file boxes. Placed on bookshelves.

Ricky wears Tony's shirts and jackets. Paul adopts two coats. Clomps around the house one day in Tony's blue suede oxfords. Too small for our towering son. We all begin using small legal tablets bought in bulk found on office shelf. I discover collection of small gifts bought but not yet given. Piled in his wardrobe. Tony thinking ahead. Paul finds book in drawer by Tony's side of the bed. Bought for him in preparation for father-son talk. *100 Questions You'd Never Ask Your Parents.*

Six months into life without Tony, sons ask me to help make Tony's favorite Filipino comfort food. Simple fare. Steaming rice fresh from rice cooker. Eggs scrambled or fried. Some sort of fried meat, whatever we have on hand. Creating large, misting plates of love. Consumed sometimes daily for weeks on end. Eaten with same tilt of head in same quiet as their father. Our sons. Two gifts. Still living.

Easter

Ricky packs for a trip to Denver on Good Friday. Road trip with friends. One I don't support. Know he continues to heal from Lyme but is not yet well. "But it's Easter!" I say.

"I forgot," he replies.

Paul leaves on school marching band trip Easter Monday. A trip we haven't really figured out. One Paul wanted to go on even back last September when no one functioned. "Do you want to go?" I asked.

"Yeh!" Paul's voice rising. "I want to go."

It's the first event Paul exhibits excitement about after Tony's death. Giving me a small, fleeting moment I hold on to for months. Most days full of negative commentary about every single aspect of life. Mysterious medical symptoms part of his every day. Making upcoming trip full of concerns. Still deciding if he will travel on bus with band or if we will fly down together. Whatever we decide, Easter weekend will be full of laundry, packing, and running errands.

My mother invites us to drive over to her church and home. An hour away. We also could travel to Chicago. Be with Tony's side of our family. But it's not a year for us to travel or to be expected to do so. It is a year for others to come to us. Some do. Some don't. "Why," I think, "do people think me capable of driving to them?"

Mom comes to us. Drags Paul to worship. He sits stiff. Missing his sibling coconspirator in all things anti-church. Leaves part way through. Gets cornered by well-meaning parishioners delighting in his presence. He, internally agonizing over how to escape.

After worship, Mom and I cook. Words few as we sprinkle shiny salmon with sea salt, lemon, and garlic. Roast some chicken breasts in olive oil, salt, and pepper. Toss asparagus spears and small red potatoes together. Cut up pears, juice beading in the bowl. Working around our collective food allergies and intolerances. Small issues compared to life's true pains.

Later we play Scrabble or cards. Sit around old oak kitchen table. Scraped up with signs of love. Remnants of over a hundred years of feeding families. Two decades of mine. Play until we feel the first Easter without Tony is over. Gotten through. Survived. Spent together, the three of us. On day signifying new life, life after death. Maybe also life after death for those of us still living.

Laughter

Eight months, one week, four days. An express mail envelope arrives. From investment company holding Tony's IRA account. Open envelope. Read handwritten note from investment advisor's assistant.

"Jennifer, I'm sorry..."

Laughter escapes my lips. For the first time in this horribly arduous process I laugh about the horribly arduous process. Because I neglected once again to sign something. Or initial something. Or plain out forgot something.

Spent hours on phone figuring out this, that, or other since Tony's death. Last September stood in social security line five times. Read documents over and over again. Unable to understand how to spend or not spend this monthly monetary saving grace. Spoke to so many retirement fund, bank, and credit card company representatives. Hearing "I'm sorry for your loss," delivered by strangers over wireless line. Quickly so as to get it over with. Followed by tagline, "We need the death certificate." That blue governmental looking piece of paper. Thick, with raised emblem. Containing words my eyes cannot bear to read.

But today laughter joins grief. There is a bit of humor here. Humor Tony would enjoy. Laughing at current state of craziness. Because Tony thought I was most funny when stressed. Now a true comedian. Funny on the outside. Ripping in pain on the inside. Surrendering today to brain on grief and in trauma recovery. Slow. Sluggish. Forgetful...sometimes funny.

Florida Front Porch

In final hours before buses full of high school students, band instruments, uniforms, and luggage pulls out of high school parking lot, Paul and I decide to fly to Florida. Stomach giving him too many twists and turns. No diagnosis. Just added frustration mixed with grief. Band directors supportive. Understanding of inability to make decisions until up against a time wall. For days, really weeks, before trip asking Paul, "Should we just fly down or do you want to take the bus?"

Paul shrugging shoulders. Me repeating question a few days later.

Sit in O'Hare airport on layover. People swirling around us. Heading south. Escaping middle America wintery spring. Lounge in plastic, sweaty row chairs as if we fly all the time at the last moment. Regardless of cost. In Orlando, follow signs to rental car desks. Pick up our compact car. Pull out of airport. Paul navigating us toward his people. Leave him at large hotel happy to see his friends. Sob driving west alone. Brief grief respite checking into hotel an hour away. Donning facade of professionalism at front desk. As if I am on a business trip. Once locked in room, crying in shower. Tears flowing again at dawn. In acute awareness of situation. Of difference between trip by myself with Tony at home working to this trip taken fully alone.

Morning brings no plans. No time at home to make any, beyond getting Paul to his rendezvous point. This morning nervously creating an agenda. Because if I don't I will sink into sorrow surrounded by chain hotel's emotionless decor. Prowl internet. Looking for place to stay near ocean. An area with a few things to do. Unable to make another decision. Call my mother. "There's this old historic inn in Gulfport..."

"Just book it," she says.

Once again compliant with other's suggestions. Reserve room, one too expensive. Repack my bag. Head out toward Tampa. Drive over long St. Petersburg bridge. Ocean surrounding me on small strip of land. Waves, seagulls, and sun welcoming me. Saying rest here for now. Find inn of forty rooms, restaurant, and large front porch through unknown streets and wrong turns. Settle into a suite dank with age, mold, and ocean air.

Sit watching street from my window. Gulfport teems with something different than Lakeland of last night. Business people replaced by vacationers and retirees. Know Tony would love this place. Off the beaten track. Touristy not commercial. Corned beef hash down the block at diner.

Ricky texts. Something about Gulfport being a great place for single mom hooligans. What does he know that I don't? Reply, "I don't hooligan."

"Good," he answers.

Continue watching from window's perch. Couples in our age range arrive two by two staying the night. Now without children. Young families in tow with snowbird parents walking beach. Grandpas with their sons, daughters, and baby grand-children parading down the street. Forcing me to bend over. Hold myself in. Miss Tony being grey haired. Carrying one of sons' children on shoulders. Talking baby talk. Emanating pride. Miss my own dad when he carried Ricky that way through Michigan woods. Miss what could have been but now will not be. Lost possibilities flowing with tears. Replaced with solitariness in strange place. Waiting for Paul. Waiting for grief to lift just a little. Waiting for some sort of sign I will again live with more joy than sorrow.

Late afternoon find refuge on inn's front porch. Enjoy bright sun from shady retreat in lazy afternoon quiet. Bend over book. Hide in biblical Hebrew verb conjugations. Another guest sits near me in wicker rocking chair. "Would you like my chair?" he asks.

"No. No thank you."

His southern accent warm and full of good manners. My lilt northern, Scandinavian, cool, private. Not interested in pleas-antries. Man in wicker chair continues, "Love this old inn. What a find. Never been to this part of St. Petersburg. I'm a pilot. Live in North Carolina. Flying out tomorrow. Just waiting for happy hour. Really waiting for happy hour. Can't wait for happy hour."

Waiting for happy hour foreign to me. Splitting a beer with friend Abbey back home is a wild night for me. Something begun after Tony died. Our favorite: cappuccino stout. Ricky finding selection wimpy. Picking out new beer for us. Settling on something brewed in St. Paul, Minnesota. (Thinking the place is in the beer's favor. Abbey and I sharing common gene pool landing in Minnesota way back when.) Not our favorite, though. Also learning to avoid lemon-infused beer. Like the one we bought at local bar. Waiting to hear Ricky's band play. Discovering it was safe sex night. Beer served with variety pack of condoms. Beer tasting like urine.

On this front porch respond to stranger's love of happy hour with nod. Eyes staying on book. Insides starting to crawl. Something vaguely familiar. Wind up of sorts. A man. A woman. Women wearing wedding ring but smelling of loneliness. He, alone. A traveler.

Pilot man gets up to take a phone call. Looking down at my book he asks, "What are you studying? Calligraphy?"

"Hebrew. I'm studying Hebrew. I'm in seminary."

Pilot man hurries away to his phone call. Of course, he must. I've said the magic words shielding me from an approaching invitation.

Sons badger me a bit about dating now and then. As months pass, this unknown makes them nervous. Many of their friends have a stepdad or a mom with revolving paramours. Some of these men are high maintenance or just not good men. I think they are wondering about my ability to choose a good partner. Maybe subconsciously thinking that choosing their dad, an excellent man, was a fluke in my female thinking.

But I am not there yet, open to another man. I am still mourning their father. Reaching for his hand each night. Crying. Grieving. However sharing our sons' trepidations about my dating future. Ability to discern a possible mate's character.

But these fears, old stuff. Left over from my twenties. The decade I dated before meeting Tony. Falling into every dating trap. Twenty-one years later and eight months into widowhood, my self-awareness, strength, and confidence crawl slowly back into my skin. Realize I have choices. The ability to be alone, rather than with someone making life emotionally harder for us. My fragility something I control. Not a state openly advertising me as easy prey. And then there's the pastor thing.

Very early into our grief, only weeks really, Paul stood in the kitchen giving me the lowdown. "I will make sure anyone you date is a good man!"

Shocked by his possessiveness, which really is his need to protect himself. "Paul, I won't be ready for a long time. I have a ton of healing to do in Dad's sudden death. And if and when I am ready, here's the deal, Paul: I'm in my fifties. Men usually look for someone three, five, ten years younger than themselves as they age. That means men in their late fifties with their eyes on retirement. I'm beginning a new career. Retirement is a long way off. And the clincher here is I'm going to be a pastor. A big, huge, and scary turnoff for a lot of men. No worries, Paul. Really."

Sarie, one of my pastor friends, maintains the ninety seconds rule. The rule goes like this: Within ninety seconds of someone learning she is a pastor, they either have some glaring emergency to attend to immediately or they dump their entire life onto her lap. Happy hour pilot sets a new speed record for this ninety seconds rule. More like thirty seconds.

Evening falls on second night. Spent sitting alone at dinner as I did the first. Both nights servers sensing pain. First night's server saying, "I bet you are not too hungry. We have wonderful appetizers though."

Hunger when it happens now is a gift. Most of the time I'm just nauseous. Stomach pressed into perpetual clench wreaking havoc on insides. My servers these nights assist appetite by practicing empathy. Food tastes delicious. Clean my plates. Neither server flinches however when discovering tears during my stay at their table. As if sobbing middle-aged women eating single is a normal experience in their line of work. Maybe it is. Maybe this little Florida hamlet shelters refugees of the heart like me. Sitting alone at candlelit tables. Full of story, chapters running down faces. Pain shedding into bread pudding, Tony's favorite dessert.

See pilot next morning at breakfast dressed in uniform. All business now with bill to pay and flight to catch. Keep my distance, guarding my pain. Laughing a bit later that of all places to stay, this one being mostly populated by couples looking for a second home, I traverse something for which I am not ready...a man.

Pick up Paul in Orlando. Feel rested. To walk along sandy ocean beaches and hike in wetland areas soothes me. Paul looks tanned. Has lots of stories. Asks for food. We fly home, grateful we came.

Healing Practice

Ongoing gifts: Our beloveds, entering into death (whatever that means) before us, leave gifts. Begin a list of these gifts. Write down big gifts like children. Write down small gifts like a favorite phrase or food. Gather these gifts together on your page.

Prayer

Lament based on Psalm 119, NRSV

"My soul clings to the dust; Revive me according to your word." (v. 25)

God, your word is love.

"My soul melts away for sorrow; Strengthen me according to your word." (v. 28)

God, your word is love.

"My soul languishes for your salvation; I hope in your word." (v. 81)

God, your word is love.

"Your word is a lamp to my feet..." (v. 105)

God, your word is love.

"Your word is...a light to my path." (v. 105)

God, your word is love. Amen.

Spring of 1997 in Tucson, Arizona, with my dad.
I am pregnant with Ricky.

Tony in college. Maybe on the Lake Michigan
shoreline around Milwaukee, Wisconsin.

V. May Days

"Give me two feeling words."
—Tony Rodriguez

Birthday

Eight and a half months. Approaching Tony's fifty-fourth birthday. Date falling on Sunday this year. During worship on previous Sunday, we hear the road to Emmaus story. My favorite story of Jesus after death. Walking alongside his friends in their pain, sorrow, and trauma. Friends pleading with this stranger, "Stay with us...it is almost evening...the day is...nearly over... "[14] They, not recognizing him or his love for them. Until breaking bread together. Jesus leaving them for second time. Two disciples walk back to Jerusalem with big news to share.

Wednesday between hearing this story and Tony's birthday, both sons break down. Become in Tony's words "activated," as in their still raw emotional wounds break open. Paul hears Tony's voice for first time in almost nine months. On video clip. One Paul took on his cell phone maybe the day before Tony died. A vacation moment captured on wooded path heading for the little farm pond. Fishing poles in hand. Tony being goofy, a dad. Captured seconds filled with laughter, joy, silliness, and future. Clip sends Paul spiraling down into his ever-present despair. Tears streaming. I sit with him in quiet. It's what Tony taught me to do. I bear witness to another's pain in holy silence. Like every parent, I want to fix this pain. But his is not mine to fix.

---

[14] Luke 24:29 (NRSV).

Paul's distress sends him back to bed and me to mine on yet another school day. In the afternoon, pick up Ricky from apartment for doctor's appointment. A few hours later, take him back with a grocery bag full of food. Late afternoon Paul reads dystopian novel. Proud of himself. Reading tenuous since tragic day at beach. For school he listens to required readings, following along in book. Today's may be the first book he's read without audio and just for his own doing. Not required. Not entertainment. Maybe escape. Call my mother. "No need to drive over. Paul's not singing in his choir concert tonight."

"Oh," she replies. Pain and worry overflowing from one syllable into silence.

Phone rings. Ricky sobbing. Ricky whom I saw only four hours ago. "Can you come get me, Mom? I'm really sad."

"I'll be right there. Are you alone?"

"No, Emily's here."

"Good."

Bolt into car. Attempt focus. Drive twenty minutes back to campus. Pick up Ricky and Emily in apartment building's grungy parking lot. Of all things overlooking a large grape arbor.

"Not here, Mom. I don't want to talk about it here," he says getting in the car.

We drive away. "When was the last time you grieved like this?"

"I don't want you to be my therapist, Mom. I want you to be my mom."

"Okay. When did you last eat?"

"I don't remember."

At home, fix him food. Laugh together as he gives me his order. Gently tease him. "I can also bake a cake or make bonbons."

"You love this, you know you do," he retorts. Feeling fully alive when my children need me even in this mess.

He eats. Finds safety on green family room couch. Same one Paul sobbed on earlier. Now game controller in hand. Emily next to him. I sit down too. "I love you." We hug. Ricky snuggles in.

House quiets. Paul sleeps. My body, full of palpable confusion and pain, slips into bed. Weighted covers keep me grounded. Heat soothes day's knotted muscles. Nod off. Wake as Ricky crawls in bed with me. "I had a flashback today."

Ah, that's why you are home. "Flashes scare and alarm us, especially at first," I whisper.

Paul's therapist told me months ago our sons may not flash back for a while. Something to do with their developing brains. Not like me, flashing within hours of the accident. "Flashbacks are the brain's way of making sense of our trauma. Your brain's telling you it's time for some mind/body trauma work like EMDR."

"I don't want to see anyone but Patrick."

"Patrick doesn't do EMDR. But Dad really liked Carol and she does EMDR." I say repeating an interchange we've had before. Add Tony's words, "Do you want to feel better or do better?"

"Maybe."

Teenagers are tricky, requiring gentle prods and pokes in moments when emotional openings allow just a bit of access. This teenager with Lyme disease causing an inflamed brain and on grief and trauma demands even more strategic moments on my parental part even in my own exhaustion and pain.

Ricky snuggles closer. "Mom, you are so strong."

Zoom in. "I'm strong now because I've been doing talk therapy, EMDR, and somatic movement therapy for months. The work of therapy strengthens me. It takes away my guilt and shame and replaces it with my own internal abilities."

No more need be said right now. Say just enough for message to stick. Repeat small messages during other unexpected moments. Always with the same goal: for Ricky and Paul to understand what has happened to us does not need to dictate the rest of our lives. "The brain continues to grow and is malleable," Tony told me again and again. During conversations when I struggled to understand how men who endured years of sexual violence as boys can heal. I ask Marit about pervasive trauma. Because my trauma is different. Yes, there are smaller traumas from my past needing healing. But Tony's death is a one-time trauma haunting me.

"When trauma has occurred multiple times, the memories merge into a few or only one main memory," she tells me. "The client does not have to use EMDR for each occurrence."

Night passes. Thursday morning Emily sounds asthmatic. "I feel like my throat is closing up," she tells us in the car. Call her mother. Drop her at door of health clinic. Ricky walks Emily to her waiting mother. Doctor agrees with my assessment. In the evening, these two fight. A big fight. Ricky drinks. Ubers home reeking of vodka. Scared about potential breakup. Too much loss for him, I think as he crawls back into bed with me. "Give Emily some time. She's sick. Whirling from that big shot of steroids the doctor gave her today. Not sleeping well because of her hacking cough."

Ricky feeling sick too. Coughing. Rub his back for bit, like I did when he was small. We both rest, the luxury of sleep not ours this night, even though he leaves his beeping phone in his bedroom for a few hours. Eventually he gets up, drives away, maybe to get Emily. They reunite in early morning hours. Ricky visibly relieved, Emily still coughing.

Early Friday morning Ricky calls again from his apartment in midst of another anxiety attack. We talk through it. He eventually sleeps, not needing to come home. Meanwhile Paul attends school on Friday. Only not going to any classes. Triggered by lecture about depression and mental illness in science class. Spends day wandering halls, in bathroom, and library. Probably doesn't want to add my maternal frustration to his day so he doesn't call.

Saturday we wait for Sunday. Mostly just wanting to get the day over with. Sunday, we plan to attend church. Eat. Go to the cemetery. Thinking beforehand it won't really happen. So many events changed or canceled because of sons' medical issues or the aftermath of Tony's death. But I need this day to happen. I need for us to be together as a family. I don't know why really. Only something about Tony's birthday is necessary for us.

Tomorrow our Chicago family keeps vigil there. Grief holding us separate. No one emotionally able to travel. All gasping for breath as if we too are caught in water's grasp. Arms flailing. Desperate to find grief's shore. They mourn the day, full of questions. We mourn the day, full of images. They cling to cultural practices for solace, many rituals about which we remain clueless. We make up our own healing needs. My cultural practices minimized or lost in sanitized European-American culture. On our first date Tony said, "Cultural traditions aren't important to me."

"Not now, but maybe in the future," I said.

Years later Tony returned with his father to the Philippines on a two-week trip. Tony seeing through adult eyes the country of his birth. Bringing back a greater understanding of his clan along with more things for our home reminding us of this part of our small family. "You were right, you know," he said without a smile. Me meeting his gaze with a nod.

Sunday, on what would have been Tony's fifty-fourth birthday, we sit in church pew. Me between our two sons. Wearing all black, Tony's wedding ring around my neck. Crying. Paul leaves service for a bit. Ricky and I hold each other. Afterwards we meet my mother for brunch. Pick out flowers at garden center. Sons choosing plants for their father's stone. Take plants to cemetery. Add more rocks to top of stone. A Jewish tradition we adopt. Dig up sod around stone in silence. Plant cacophony of mixed-up color. Add some mulch. Water. Eyes remain dry.

Lead up to Tony's birthday joins growing group of "first anniversary issues." Marit tells me body just knows. Remembers in fibers buried deep within. Surfacing to skin in days before holidays, birthdays, death days. As if entering an emotional time warp. Catapulting us back into shock, fear, horror, sorrow, loss, and devastation. A time of strapping in, buckling up, riding it through. Days before far worse for me than the day itself.

Temperatures soar after Tony's birthday, into nineties with no rain. Dust blows across fields as farmers till and plant. Sinuses clog, sending us to cupboard for pain relief and allergy medication. Some combination of us stops at cemetery almost daily to water new plantings. Begin recognizing twisting route in and out to Tony's grave. Enter off small brick-paved street called Brown. Onto narrow cemetery road. Drive past caretaker's cottage, Civil War private, famous, looming, dangerous black angel, gazebo memorial honoring organ donors, famous artist's sculpture. Weaving right at adjoining park's trees and trailhead. Park across from non-potable water spigot. Sons' irritation mounting each visit with reminders of water being non-drinkable. Motherly repetition no longer necessary.

The Sunday after Tony's birthday, stop here after celebrating Mother's Day. Site looks tended, creative, a bit funky. "You are well-loved, Tony."

Talk Therapy

Marit asks, "Do you still talk to Tony?"

"Not much."

Should I be talking to him? I don't talk to him really. Not enough, I guess. Oh God! I'm not a good widow. I was not a good wife. What would I say if I did talk to him?

Thoughts spill out. Hidden beneath nervous chatter. Truth stuffed into middle of topical conversation. Like the ham found inside Norwegian dumplings. Talk, talk, talk until I say, "My sons spend an entire day grieving and then days or weeks not grieving at all. I spend of few minutes to an hour every day grieving in some form of highly efficient grief."

She laughs. Maybe it's a therapist thing because Tony would have laughed at my assessment as well—right at this point in our conversation. "What is it about you therapists?"

Marit's response to my perpetual self-analysis brings me closer to Tony than talking to him does right now. Or maybe talking to Marit is a stand-in for talking to Tony. An earthly substitution. Tony, like Marit, suppressed smiles during my verbal tirades. "Why are you laughing?" I'd ask him. "Why are you laughing at my anger?"

Marit knows that I read Tony's cowritten book, *Facing Heartbreak: Steps for Recovery for Partners of Sex Addicts*. That I do the exercises. I wonder which ones Tony created. Look for relief in his work. Today she quickly quiets her laughter. Shares a meditation chant with me. While I sit on her ugly, sagging brown couch. Something about breathing in goodness and breathing out pain. Then she says, "Heartbreak is an opening within us. This opening allows people and stuff in. Some of what wants to come in is not good for us. We need gatekeepers. People guarding our tender and healing hearts. Allowing only the good stuff in like love, light, hope, and mercy."

She's not normally this verbose. But her voice remains soft, quiet. Her gaze intent. Words catching my attention, making sense. Marit is one of my gatekeepers. Keeping bad stuff at bay. For us. For Tony. Thinking how many people are in my life now after Tony's death. Feeling maybe these people were always there but I didn't or couldn't see them. Why did it take tragedy for me to see?

I go home. To talk to Tony.

Parenting

In grieving nights my mind asks the air, "What do my children need?"

Air repeating, "Love. They need love."

Love not simple ever. Not now. Not during grief's aching sadness and trauma's reactions. Love active though. Reminding our sons of my love for them. Their dad's love for them. Again and again love sitting in silences between us. Acknowledging both pain and healing. Love "bearing witness," as Tony said.

Love gently poking at teenage resistance. "Maybe more mindbody work will help."

"It didn't work the first time. I'm not going back!"

"Numbing out with video games makes things worse. Prolongs the healing."

"Yeh, yeh, yeh."

Life overwhelming. Attempt to love. Love myself, sons, God. Love the only verb left.

Journal Entries

May 6, 2017.

Overwhelming needs in grief. Heard in voices. My mother spinning on and on about our trip this summer. Ricky's muscles spasming at 5:30 this morning. Mother-in-law's sadness on phone. Paul's frustrations with ongoing medical mysteries. Me, point person in everyone's sorrow.

Arms ache again today. Just ache because I ache inside and out. Head hurts. Feet hurt. Cheeks flush red with exhaustion. What doesn't ache tingles with tiny pinpricks. My body riddled by invisible points of pain.

May 10, 2017. Signs everywhere. Warnings for others. Where is our sign? Grieving, traumatized humans. Proceed with compassion.

Nine Months

In my journal I write, "Nine months tomorrow. Am road weary. No oasis in sight. Done with grief. Done with trauma recovery. Neither done with us."

Put down pen. Settle into covers. Close eyes. The beach scene replays. Runs through body. The one taking Tony away from us. "Stop!" I tell it.

Scene listens. Next morning, I sleep in. Added rest with a side of nightmare. Dream filled with water. Push nightmare aside. Make breakfast moving to Israeli music. Bacon sizzling to its beat. Paul's chocolate chip waffles steaming on iron. Mothering on this day before Mother's Day.

Think of Miriam's celebratory joy. At river when baby brother Moses finds safety in arms of Pharaoh's daughter. Same joy Miriam shows in tambourine and dance. After crossing parted Red Sea. Into safety from slavery. Before forty years of wandering. "Sing to the LORD," she calls.[15] My heart answers, "Yes, sing to the LORD!"

We walk far and wide in grief and trauma's desert. Making way toward promised healing. Traveling day after day. Traversing uncharted lands. No distant end point visible. This morning rejoicing in accomplished miles. Singing praises to universe, God, therapists, friends, family, pastors. Nine months today!

After breakfast, think back to morning's dream. In it, my friend David, a therapist, becomes a real estate agent. Shows me lake home at dusk. Afterwards we wade into lake up to our chests. Others do the same. I wear a life vest. David does not. Feel pull of water against vest. Tugging. Asking me forward. Light wanes. Can barely see. David becomes a shadow. Slips underwater. Call out, "David?"

No answer. Not again, I think. I can't do this again.

---

[15] Exodus 21:15 (NRSV).

I wake up. Shaking. Sweating. Heart pounding. Orient myself by staring at walls of bedroom. Breathe in relief. Breathe out terror. Remember that the mind is a tricky thing. Bringing back what I do not wish to recall, ever. A moment in a day when life changed with no warning. Inner workings of nervous system telling me at nine months more healing yet to be done with more therapy.

On day of widowing, waited only two, maybe three hours. Thinking nine months later how added nightmare of waiting overnight or night after night at rented farm house unbearable. Wandering property in haze. Scraps of hope teasing my heart. Watching. Praying. Finally seeing truck drive up lane. Knowing. Truths understood before words spoken.

Grateful Tony's body, although blue and swollen, was still a body I could hug. Hold. His arms still strong as if ready to hold me once again. His face, as if napping, one I recognized. Beautiful hair I could caress. A body open for viewing later in week. Vestiges of drowning death gone or covered up. Only four of us knowing what he looked like after being found by divers.

Nine months. I still ache everywhere. Gasp for air. Flail for safe footings or hands to hold. I'm tired of pain. Tired of grief. Want so very much to share burdens with a partner but really just with Tony. "It's already nine months," my mother-in-law tells me. Implying she wants us to care for her. We cannot comply. Our pain, trauma, and grief continues. No new birth in sight.

Mother's Day

Mother's Day. First without man who made me one. Wake in tears. Drive to Moline, Illinois, where I was born. Where my mother lives. Where Paul was born. Where the Mississippi River bends forming hills and valleys smelling of woods and mud, air thick with water particles, bald eagles soaring, sky expanding. Where Tony insisted we move. Living twelve years on Iowa's side. The place I pined for in first hours without Tony.

Paul laughs with Ricky. Ricky laughs with Paul. Banter spreading balm. I smile upon them. Wanting so very much to hold them close. Hold on to them so nothing awful and horrible ever happens again. Tell them I love them every minute. Knowing words can never express how complete I am because of them. Because my body grew them, birthed them, nursed them, held them, and now watches them in their illnesses, grief, and trauma.

Some boys played and swam in the Wisconsin River that day near Tony, Ricky, and Paul. Saw them as I walked toward my beloveds in confusion. Someone's sons playing among scene of happy people. Their presence forming part of my disbelief in what was happening.

Some other boys run along beach following current as it takes my beloveds away. Shout out instructions: how to break the current by swimming sideways. Paul tells me this later. Months later as I piece together how the river pushed them out. Down toward the bridge. With no one noticing, caring—except these children doing the work of adults. Because so many people on the beach or in boats were living in their own little worlds.

Someone's sons saved my sons' lives that day. Not in a boat or with a thrown flotation device. But with information. Which my sons followed. Ricky exhausted from swimming against the current trying to escape in a burst of adrenaline. Paul exhausted from treading water. Both somehow able to do as they were told. Something Tony could not do in shock, terror, fatigue.

Thoughts shake me. Admitting what might have been. Losing Tony rips my heart apart. Losing my sons as well, a total shredding of heart, soul, and mind. Into too many particles. Too many to collect and reform.

With my mother, we mark this day in a restaurant full of dining families honoring mothers. Sun shining. Temperature, a balmy sixty-five degrees Fahrenheit. Yet in my unseen heart's beat we celebrate life. My children facing me in a dark booth in a nice restaurant. Eating with no manners. Salmon, new potatoes, roast beef, warm dinner rolls, fresh fruit. Commenting on the food, "Well, it's not the Outing Club but it's good."

"I'm going back for more cake."

"These rolls are great!"

Eating. Overeating. Even me. Not sitting in front of two or three graves. Weeping. Convulsing in agony. Alone. Even if with people. Here in this place today. Acknowledging my mother, who gave me life, and the two best gifts Tony ever gave me.

Journal Entries

May 16, 2017.

"Not tonight," I order the flashback again. "I want to sleep."

May 18, 2017 at 9:22 p.m.

I have a full life because you loved me first when I was lost. Finding me in your own version of life's "lost & found" box. A stray looking for a home, a home you built for us, with me.

You loved me in our imperfect yet human love. Through my anxieties, shyness, and fears compounded by years of wandering. You loved me and I stand today facing a new "come what may." Bound to beautiful sons and people because of you. You loved me into my true me. Me still here in our life created together living on.

Brain Back

Thinking again. In brain's best driver's seat, frontal lobe. Confronted by how far down in brain's inner workings I lived these past months. Slogging through soggy mire. Bogged down in overriding emotions. Operating in brain's stem. Therapy releasing me into emotional arena, the amygdala and other accompanying areas. Now once again thinking inside my forehead. Not all day. Not like before. But enough to give me hope. Movement within brain producing tomorrow. Reminded of Tony's words as his head fell on pillow after long, hard day. "Tomorrow's a new Lutheran day."

Took survey at seminary identifying what talents could morph into strengths. Of my top ten talents, five fall in category of strategic—strategic, intellectual, learner, idea person, resourceful. New knowledge empowers me. Because being strategic means creating alternatives when not knowing how to carry on in life. And mostly I don't know how to carry on.

Yet something's missing from survey. Brain's dormancy in trauma's aftermath. Called an immobility response. Kind of living death. Like animals averting predators by using profound motionlessness.

Frontal lobe's strategic strengths inaccessible in trauma's immediate wake. Initial shock keeping my brain stem-bound in the most ancient part of this organ. Creating frozen, slow-motion state. Hardly breathing. After six to eight weeks in shock, grief detaining my soul in swirling, activated emotions. Ones I can't even name. Shown in tears, escaped sighs, breath sucked in escaping through pursed lips. Paul complaining more than once, "Stop blowing on me!"

With clinical work, brain moving back into forehead. Returning in increments for brief visits. Inner senses beginning behind eyes becoming words vocalizing from mouth. Current and future plans finding pen and forming on scraps of paper.

Still moments of forgetfulness haunt me. Bills left unpaid. Haircut missed. Emails unread or worse deleted. Words when speaking to others escape between thought and formation. Unable to even make a daily "to do" list.

Tony and I created our own verb for brain stem behavior. We called it "stemming," as in "Paul is stemming. I think he's overtired."

Or during the time when our oldest son suffered from unrecognized Lyme disease we asked each other, "Why does Ricky stem so much into rages?"

Stemming, as a term, is similar to Tony's other clinical slang word: spinning. Stemming surfaces when basic needs for food, sleep, or safety go unfulfilled. Or illness sets in or is already present. Or as in my case trauma occurs. Settling in for an extended brain stay. Spinning has roots in anger, grief, sadness, and other emotional triggers. That weird energy making all of us seemingly super productive when upset, over-tired, angry. Sort of like the second wind older people speak of.

First days after Tony's death I remember stemming and spinning. Spinning through death's business. Stemming in tearful rants. Stemming feeling like deer in headlights. Or as Pastor Peter said at Tony's funeral, "Folks, this family feels like a lion. Stunned by the chair legs jabbed into its face by the circus trainer."

Paul speaks of my disappearance after Tony died. Of my body in the house, the rest of me—heart, soul, and mind—scattered across the prairie. For months daily collecting pieces of the one I once was. Filling life's basket. Bit by bit. "I felt like I lost both my parents," he tells me.

I return enough for Paul's words to slash into me. Into my slowly healing self. "I had no one," he continues. Giving me his pain.

Receiving it as his parent. His only living parent. Want to defend myself and perhaps I do before catching my words. Allowing Paul his truth. Pray my admission allows for his healing. "I'm sorry," I reply.

"I'm sorry Paul," I repeat. "I wasn't there for you. I wish I could have been."

Remember all the meals I fed him afterwards. Soggy mashed potatoes. Overcooked, unseasoned pork chops. Greens dumped out of a bag and into a bowl. Store bought rotisserie chicken. Dry frittatas. Paul surveying plate. Disgust forming on face. Sighing, "More dead Dad food."

Me not responding. Paul noticing lack of food on my plate. "Do you have an eating disorder?"

Yes, I think. It's called trauma.

Meals provided for us during the first two months. Set at our doorstep or handed over. Sight of food nauseating. Smells aversive. Stomach clenching. Acts of love by others not enough to make us eat. From November on taking over the cooking. Sort of. Not really. Barely. Fridge often bare. Me living on carbonated water and chocolate. Now not remembering at all what Ricky ate. Paul picking at rotisserie chicken. Eating crackers instead. Unless a friend dropped by her famous pumpkin bars. Then Paul feasted.

Days and nights attempting check-ins with Paul. Walking into his room. Knowing I wasn't welcomed. Not knowing what to do or how to do it. "How are you doing?"

"Fine."

A masking word saying nothing.

Another time Paul saying, "I need to have some fun."

Finds drone online. Thousand dollars. How can I say "no" to my child living in misery? My mother gives him money. I give him money. Paul buys drone. Small flickering light amidst daily wounds.

My brain's behavior made for a second death of sorts for all of us. Not a mom during those early days and months. Paul zeroing in on truth. With razor edges of teenage observation. Cutting through all my human layers. The reality: I could not parent. I was not there for him. This fact now mine to work out in therapy as I reinstate myself fully as his mother. If he allows me. If his trust in me is not fully broken. If I can stay the course. If I can love through pain.

Slow.

"Love you, mom."

"I love you too."

Ricky gathers a bag of groceries from back seat. Slams car door. Sends me his standard parting. Heads into his apartment. First college semester ended a week ago. Now he scrambles to find summer employment. Hangs out at home a bit more when he can get a ride or convince me to come get him.

My children settle my soul. Their light brown eyes focusing. Their hair, the same color as their eyes, growing oh so long. Lush for one, curly for the other. Their distinct smells and habits. The little sounds they make while living. A cough, sigh, laugh. Ricky, heavy-footed. Paul, lighter. Timbre of voices the same. Paul, analytical. Ricky, emotional. Both creative.

Tonight, a car ride together with my oldest son. Quietly chatting about little things. A future doctor's appointment. Grocery items asked for. The next time he'll be home. Drop him off.

Drive home alone as darkness descends on day. Through winding roads. Car windows open. Smell of lilacs floating on air. Deer out foraging for food. Folks sitting on porches. Dusk creating balm. Allowing me to say, "I can do this. I can do this life well."

Brace for flowing tears, shaking horror, body wails. Tony's absence running me over once again. But tonight for entire drive home I am only and merely and surprisingly happy.

Flashbacks

Almost June yet scenes still blankets nights. Replayed when weary head finds pillow or jolted awake at three. Repeat of Tony's death day. Flashback in unwanted reiteration. Sounding alarm. Signaling need. Time to collect more story's fragments, one by one, like puzzle pieces. Pull pieces together with care. Until thorough narrative emerges.

Last moment I saw Tony alive: I'm in the water. Walking toward Tony. Wondering what is going on. River rising with every step. Up to my waist. Then higher. To my chest. Current pushing me. Pulling me. Something wrong. Terribly wrong. Frightfully wrong. Water's strong arms embrace my beloved. Engulf him like a lover. Tony slips under the water in graceful movement. As if completing a dance move. Making no sense.

I am voiceless for what seems like a day or forever or eternity. Time halting. Freezing. Allowing shock a passageway into my soul. Call out to man in boat. Fishing boat with small motor. A dingy. Large blond man springs into some sort of slow-motion action. A firefighter on his day off. Tells someone to call 911.

I stare at water where Tony went under. Where he no longer is. Asking for him to emerge eyes squeezed shut, mouth clenched, water spewing off his back, popping out of the water like he used to when playing with our sons. But it's as if he evaporated right before my eyes like a magic trick, a joke, a bit of teasing—that's only fun for the teaser.

Ricky grabs our kayak. Paddles furiously down the river with the current. Without a life vest. I turn to young man near me. "Follow him with a life vest," I say.

Paul disappears into beach full of people. Sits with our family who carry on with the day because they do not know. Learn later he tells my brother some "guy" is drowning. Shock speaking for him. No one helping him because no one knows. A man walks up to Paul later. Telling him he did the right thing by breaking the current. So it seems some people did know my family was in danger. Why no one took action besides children, I do not know. Not knowing blasts my heart apart again and again and again. Forever.

I hear for the first time "five minutes." The amount of time a person can typically survive underwater without dying or maybe it's significant brain damage. Can't remember. Ricky returns from fight-or-flight trip downriver. Paul texts his cousin Joe. Ricky calls Tony's dear friend, a therapist.

I climb out of the water onto a patch of sand. A young couple surrounds me as I kneel, too dizzy to stand. Still staring at the spot where I last saw Tony. They pray. I stare. A toddler dances in front me. Mind absorbs the rope with attached life ring that the man holds as he prays.

Called away. To speak with someone in charge. Because we require someone to be in charge. He asks questions I do not know how to answer. About Tony's swimming ability. His name. My name. Where we live. Information I thought private.

Wait at a hastily chosen ground zero. A patch of thin grass near the beach maybe under a tree or two. Near ambulance. Kneel on the ground. Ground keeping me safe. Cannot think or speak. Cold. Remain cold for hours in hot sun. Mom finds me. Asks first responders for a blanket. Tries to keep herself together for me as our world falls apart. Blanket arrives. Wrap myself in it. Waiting. Shivering. Thirsty. Frozen. Scared. Touching the ground. Always touching the ground. As close to the earth's life as can be.

See Tony's body before the team erects flimsy privacy screen covering him and their work. See rescue boat, Tony's purple legs, and the blue of his swim shirt. Recognize him in the way he is splayed on the gurney. Feet turned outward as if taking a nap on our bed. Relieved he is back near us. Hold no hope of life's force rushing through him. Even I know time is not on the side of our desperate desires.

Told by man in charge that the rescue team attempts resuscitation following protocol. Chances slim. Within minutes, time of death called. Coroner lies in wait. Emerges from a car. Approaches me. Our old life, the one with which we arrived here at this place today in hopes of a restful, fun day full of joy, officially fades. Replaced by stark reality, shock, pain, trauma, grief. Without my permission. Without my control. Without my willingness. Without my agreement. Without Tony.

Layers

First post-accident Eye Movement Desensitization Recovery (EMDR) sessions occur months after Tony's death. After diminishing shock makes way for grief allowing sleep to lengthen and a small range of emotions to return. First waves of healing making me ready to make sense of and discard internal felt senses of trauma's chaos for a chance to live.

Marit prompts me to return. Back to the day, to the beach. Not to the story. But to my questions. "Why couldn't I save him? Why didn't I read the green-yellow-red sign tucked away under the trees? Why didn't I remember the soft warning in the tourist booklet? Why?"

Hands me two small, grey pods. One pod for each of my palms. Gentle buzz of small, medical-looking, EMDR machine vibrates through pods. Left. Right. Left. Right. Left. Right. Marit adjusts vibration speed. Until it mirrors my musical heart. Left. Right. Left. Right. Underlying beat accompanies single part of that day. As I remember it. Body tingling in cheeks, arms, nose, and neck. Word by word, buzz by buzz, brain lets go of something. Freeing me from within just a bit.

Tony loved EMDR. Before the days of the EMDR machine, he complained of finger fatigue. Using his pointer finger in a left, right motion a few feet in front of participating client's face. Client following his finger with their eyes. Tony, marveling at how well the technique worked in our evening catch-up conversations while rubbing his sore finger. Me wondering if fingers can develop repetitive motion issues.

When I asked Tony about a therapist the spring before his death, one who could help me with my emotional fatigue surrounding sons' combined illnesses, he suggested Marit. Because he respected her, thought she was well-trained, and certified in EMDR, which in Tony's mind meant she was up on the latest research and techniques. I learned to trust Marit with my shame. In turn she continues to help roll away my unhealthy guilt. Revealing hidden sheaths of skin holding on to emotional chaos. Session by session dissolving layers. Relieving my heart. Releasing small bits of new life.

Marit takes me through all moments of that day. Bit by bit. Month by month. EMDR session by EMDR session on days when my heart can take it. Other times, offloading my stress onto this living saint. In another session on another day, a loud "NO" erupts deep within me. Word I was unable to say when Tony slipped under the water. Word imploding instead throughout my body. Lodging everywhere like shrapnel. Ringing through muscles, organs, and neural pathways for months. The word so lost within me it couldn't find a way out.

My somatic movement therapist, Meg, on the other side of town reenacts my "NO!" Her body stiffening. Palms facing outward with hands jerking up toward shoulders. Movement taking upper back, shoulders, and head back.

As I witness my hands fly up. Cover mouth. Catch cry in recognition. "You had a startle reflex," she says. "It turned inward. Creating a stuck adrenaline loop along your upper back and through your arms."

Meg works out the stuck adrenaline session by session. Yet as months accumulate, aching reignites in arms' vulnerable areas in times of added stress. Meg teaches me to break this unwanted returning visitor by arching my back over a small, slightly deflated exercise ball. "Arching," she says, "empowers us."

I understand that two people, Marit and Meg, set me free. Because that is what they do for me, for others. Like Tony did. Their expertise and experience understands that my stuck "NO" did not fully dissipate into earth's atmosphere upon initial release. Eradicating all trauma's shame and pain. Fully freeing me. Marit continues asking me to return to that day. Now resisting a bit. Tired of doing this healing work. But trust her. Once again speak my feelings of isolation that afternoon. "Where was the help? Why was there no lifeguard? Why were so many people on the beach and in the water? No one understanding what was happening to Tony, Ricky, Paul?"

Alternating buzz of EMDR machine opens into tiny specks of forgiveness for these strangers. But not much. Then experience sons' trauma. Something my brain knew but body could not feel. Not until between buzzes, I see them coming out of the water, walking like stone pillars, heading away from their dad. Today feeling flooded with their fear. Sobbing for them, my beloveds, while sitting in the middle of Marit's saggy brown sofa. Marit's quiet voice again saying, "Go back to the scene." Followed by a deep breath and her eyes closing. Machine humming. Buzzing in my palms. Left. Right. Left. Right. I stare at the wall. Look through the ocean beach photo hanging there. See scene unfold again. Built on months of collecting its pieces. Rebuilding them into a story.

Shoulders collapse, heavy from carrying our world. Let go of responsibility not mine to carry: that of making river's dangers known to all. Thinking I must do this task. Future deaths on me instead of those truly responsible. Somehow associated again with my own guilt. Making myself the responsible party in Tony's death and in all future deaths. That weight finally lifted off me with a breath emanating from my toenails, catapulting me back into life.

Left. Right. Left. Right. Left. Right. Alternating buzzes reconnect my synapses. Release my breath. Lift some of guilt's weight. Freeing me to live.

Another day I am again thinking I am finally done with EMDR, that I've healed sooner than anticipated, being a good student of trauma recovery. Life moving on now without baggage. Marit suggests, "Let's try it again. Let's see if we have it all."

Groan. Follow her lead. Volume turned to five. Intensity turned to five. Speed at five as well. Left. Right. Left. Right. Left. Right. Back into one moment. The moment I lost Tony. Marit asking again and again, "What do you feel in your stomach?"

Left to right, left to right. Remains of something I can only describe as a clenched ball filling up my stomach releases. In doing so, something permeates my being. I am sad. Quietly, deeply, and completely sad. I look at Marit in recognition. "This sadness is what I couldn't feel at the beach," I say.

She nods. It's what she's been after all along. Unearthing the seed of my pain. It's why Tony thought highly of her skills. Because like him she was willing to sit through the entire process in order to find truth's entirety, bearing witness to both my experience and the lengthy healing process.

Deeper than tears, sadness slows me. Wraps me in its arms. Stays with me for days. Not evil or gut-wrenching, but quiet, beautiful, like a lover's arms wrapped around me as light dawns on a new day. Maybe Tony's arms holding me in his own grief. Maybe God's sadness too. But I don't remember God at the beach. Clung to the ground. Shivering. Still wet from being in the water. Too stunned to bargain. Calling out to God, earth, anyone listening for mercy.

Marit pulls away layer after layer revealing cavernous depths of sorrow and pain. Gifts me with my sadness. Not gut-wrenching wailing pain or steady stream of tears or heavy weight of depression. Marit's craft allows me to gather in my sadness, to combine it with Tony's and the boys', and yes, God's. And in doing so to recognize this sadness as love. My love. Tony's love. Our sons' love. God's love. Finally hearing, experiencing, the compassion I begged for on the beach. Hunched over the ground. Hugging it. Internally wrenching. Afraid to let go.

Healing Practice

Breathe in with slowness naming wonderful and good stuff in your life. Allow these things to float into you through oxygen. Breathe out with same slowness naming yucky, bad stuff in your life. Allow these things to float out of you through carbon dioxide.

Prayer

"By the tender mercy of our God, the dawn from on high will break upon us, to give light to those who sit in darkness and in the shadow of death, to guide our feet into the way of peace."[16]

God of all dawns, bring forth a new day for me, for us, for all who are in pain. Guide our feet into the way of peace. Amen.

Young Tony with his family in the Philippines circa 1966.

On our swing set in Davenport, Iowa, in 2002.

---

[16] Luke 1:78–79 (NRSV).

Last photo of Tony and Riphanie taken in July 2016 in Chicago, Illinois.

VI. Beautiful Mess

"Home is where we do the hard stuff."[17]
— Tony Rodriguez

Road Trips

Heat soars, pushing one hundred degrees Fahrenheit though it's not even summer yet. Feel hot from inside my bones. Driving worn routes. Passing small Iowa towns sprouting corn or beans, blowing wind farms, and leftover election signs. Left arm tingles from too much sun pouring in driver's window. Crank volume on tunes staying awake by singing into lulling afternoon warmth.

At Interstate 35 turn north. Temperature drops at Minnesota's border. Car cools as does my head. By Lakeville, thermometer reads seventy-five with relief. Brain clears in parking lot of a Super Target. Just in time for hardest part of day's travels to begin. It is almost ten months since Tony died.

Five weeks after Tony died I drove to Minnesota for the first time. Longtime editors in Minneapolis arranged a two-day meeting with partnering organization on a project brand I love. Knew project was coming before Tony died. Had emails in inbox about it. Thought meeting later in fall. Or perhaps hoped my participation passed over due to our unforeseen circumstances.

---

[17] A number of authors refer in their written work and videos to doing hard work. Brené Brown does. Glennon Doyle does. From where Tony's quote originates, I do not know. What I do know is that from an attachment theory point of view we work through our love relationships, both old and current, in order to heal. And this work is home work.

But emails kept coming in early September of our grief. Thought we needed money. Desperate for anything from old life. Anything once thought normal. Anything I once enjoyed. Said "yes." Work, after thirty-five days into despair, an escape from the sorrow emanating from every wall of our home.

My mother moved in for a few days. Waved as I drove out of town. Tears drenching face. Body shaking. Hand hitting steering wheel again and again. Soul screaming, "Where are you?"

Lost sense of direction in otherwise familiar suburban Bloomington, Minnesota. But grief's confusion laced with night, adding an extra hour onto angst.

Collapsed in hotel room, alone. Body pounding. First time away from sons since that day. Day Tony died. Ordered room service. Plates, bowls, utensils scattered about. Food picked at until cold and coagulated. Attempted sleep. Missed Tony in emptiness of room. Talked to him for first time in our five-week-old mess. Words punctuated by sobs. "Miss you. Wish you were here. With me. Now."

Next morning sat stunned in meetings. Cloaked in black. Squeaking out comment here. There. Confused. Splintered. Asked editor. "Why did you ask me here? I am so broken." Words met by silence. Hand placed on upper back. With love and tenderness. Steering me into elevator toward day's work. Drove home next afternoon sobbing the entire five-hour trip. Know from texts that my absence is hard for sons. Guilt smeared onto pain.

In November travel to Minnesota again. On federal election day with Ricky and Paul. Three months after Tony's death. To see their functional medicine doctor. In little town outside St. Cloud, Minnesota. Line at voting polls too long for Ricky to vote for the first time before we need to leave. I voted absentee weeks before, but forgot to sign my name, adding yet another trip to county building. Place I now know well. Moving names on car registrations part of widow's job.

Drive with dry eyes. Boys sleep for first half of trip. Wake as we turn from interstate onto two-lane highways. Day crisp and clear. Crops in. Dust settling. Fields tan and brown again. Countryside filled with flatbed trucks boasting Trump signs. Boys make fun. We laugh. Laughter carries us through another three hours of travel.

Spend long hours at doctor's office. Drive back into Twin Cities for night. Pull into hotel. One Paul found for us next to Mall of America. Place bubbles with excitement and reporters. Front desk clerk keeps source of activity close to her vest. Figure out we are staying at hotel hosting the Minnesota Republican's election party.

We hide away. I steam up bathroom with a long, hot shower. Paul reads or watches something. Ricky roams hotel gathering data. Reports back to us in intervals. Wakes me late with final results as building erupts in choir of combined celebratory human voices.

Morning. Friends plummet into despair. Online fury falling everywhere. I remain numb. Still fragile. Collapsed internally. Heart rate signaling lack of oxygen. Election results exist in haze. Find sun's warmth in bank of dining room windows. Eat expensive oatmeal. Look up from newspaper. See man carrying life size photo blow-up of now president-elect Trump. Wide grin covering man's face. Some sort of pride or triumph. Pair, seated together for breakfast. Text friend Sarie. In need of communion. She wants photo. Ask waitress, "Do you think I can take a photo?"

"Obviously he wants attention," she says topping off my tea.

Sons laugh at morning adventure. Shop while I walk the mall. Afterwards clambering into car. Driving homeward as unaccustomed laughter mingles with smells of teenage boys. Smiles and laughter no longer normal. Reemergence welcomed. Small break from all we've been through, blanketing us from the day's realities. Our private experience a stark contrast to the nation's day of collective celebration or deep dread.

Mid-January. Five months a widow. Travel again. Overnight trip to Twin Cities. Left nephew in charge. Worry replaced tears as I drove. Reassured myself, "They'll be fine. They will be fine."

Which is a lie or projection. Because I know all can go wrong. In an instant.

Stay with Aunt Linda. Support of another sudden widow needed. Given in hugs, listening soul, and repeated words normalizing pain and strength. "You are strong," she says. "You can do this."

Attend first dinner of seminary class at Luther Seminary in St. Paul, Minnesota. Make small talk. Realize how many people do not know of our tragedy. Or don't connect news of last August with me. Or freeze in not knowing what to say. Grief and trauma unwelcomed here for reasons unknown to me. Unmooring me in place far from home's safety. Why did I come? I wonder.

Next day lunch with the two longtime editors. Restaurant housed in reclaimed old bank building in downtown Minneapolis. Filling me up with food and support and love. Leave lunch with a sense of joy, having experienced goodness. Walk to car in gentle flurry of snowflakes, smiling. Ask car park ticket man, "What's the weather supposed to do?"

"Snow," he says cracking a small smile or matching mine.

Flurries turn into storm. Two and one-half hours later, I'm only in the outer suburbs of the Twin Cities. Press on. Wanting desperately to be home. Hear sounds of sons. Hide away from life moving on within others' realities.

By Albert Lea, southern border between Minnesota and Iowa, even truck drivers quit. Find hotel right off interstate. Collapse. Grateful I did not die on icy treacherous roads. Dread always right there now. Fear something will happen to me. Cannot happen to me. Hypervigilant in my personal safety. Call home. "Joe, I can't make it home tonight. The roads are awful."

"It's alright, Aunt Jennifer. I just need to leave by noon."

Sleep until dawn. Waking every hour. Hotel emanating sounds of weary travelers coming in all night long. Leave early next morning after sneaking into unopened breakfast area. Helping myself to tea and granola bars. Starting car with plea. "Please, God. Let me get home safely. Please don't let me die."

Now early June. Today, fourth widowed trip to Minnesota. Approaching ten months. Drinking water in Lakeville, Minnesota, parking lot. Steeling myself for rest of today's trip.

In days prior, fill refrigerator and freezer with food options. Lack of food was sons' complaint about my other trips. Uttered by people not eating much. Food symbolic. Of home. Hearth. Security. Love. Also write lists and notes and arrange schedules. Prepare for intensive seminary class. Work ahead on writing project. Flashbacks dull, recede, or just don't bother me. Feel good for an entire week.

Transitions, I remind myself with some prior wisdom, are always the hardest time in life. Most telling of our emotional health as individuals and families. My trips are transitions for all of us. Small upheavals in current routine. But loss and grief, the real transition. Changes in every daily nuance. Leaving us scrambling for reestablishment of predictability. Life moving. Never stopping. From then, now. Toward what? Cannot tell or figure out or fully know.

At dusk this day, move into dorm room. Settle into hot, third floor space. No air conditioning. Feel invisible in this new place. Pain not knowing how to speak or feel or be truthful here. Want to return home. To safety. Crawl back into bed where human dynamics of strangers not welcomed. Hide under covers. In sacred space. Writing, my coping mechanism. Necessary for functioning. Paul texts a few days into separation. "Can you come home?"

"If you really need me to, I will."

Make promise. Which gets harder to keep as week goes on and end of class nears. Wonder if he just wants to know when or whether he really needs me to come home. Feel guilty all over again. For leaving them for an entire week. For being a crappy mother all these many months. For not being able to save their father. For closing Tony's business. For beginning seminary. So many guilts. So many, many guilts. "Just wondering when," he tells me later, crisis passed.

Make new friend. Laura quiet, unassuming. Her compassion folding into my angst. Offers calm, not advice. Finds me before dinner each night. Eats with me. Talking slowly. Meet another new friend, Patricia. Face etched with beautiful crevices. Revealing life lived in full feeling. Heart hugging sudden loss of daughter-in-law. Listening to my ramblings when really needing to write a paper. "Why am I even here? No one understands grief or trauma! I need to go home."

"It will get better. When, I can't tell you. Just that it will."

Solace freely given by two people a week ago strangers. As grief and trauma walk before me. My rawness bumping into most others. Except these two.

Early each morning walk surrounding streets of seminary. Neighborhood called St. Anthony Park. Some sort of cruel joke on my ripped open heart. Homes sit on top of small hills. Amidst winding roads, towering trees, and overgrown succulents, hosta plants. School and an old-fashioned walkable shopping district a block or two away. Creating a small urban town. Housing stock glaringly out of price range for us. Yet Tony would have dreamed of living here. Yearned for it. Worked for it. Loved it. Midweek I say to universe, "It's ten months today."

Sob through chapel, making all future pastors uncomfortable except the few with innate pastoral care sensibilities. There's a service of healing this day. My academic advisor lays her hands on me and prays. Know immediately this woman is an amazing conduit of God's love. Able to hold my pain. Not make it her own. Allow space between us. Liminality required for healing to stick.

Rest of my time at seminary half there. Functioning numb.

Ship Trip

A few weeks later we board a cruise ship with Tony's side of our family in Fort Lauderdale, Florida. Walk beach before boarding. Notice large signs in black, white, and red where water meets sand. The day's water safety level shown using different colored flags attached to the signs. Explanations of water's possible dangers for tourists. One community's care shredding my stomach. So simple, I think. Simple, logical solutions. Communicating possible danger. Why not in Wisconsin?

Beautiful Mess

Return from Florida and the Bahamas. Only to leave again for Minneapolis. Fifth Minnesota trip in the eleven months since Tony died. New writing project available. Want the work. Need the work. Choice in matter, a luxury I do not have. No time to find someone to stay with Paul. Ricky moving out of his apartment. Home most of the time. A year into Lyme recovery and eleven months into trauma and grief healing, he is well enough to seem responsible and present.

Not enough to soothe my anxieties, so I leave rattling off reminders left and right. List of people to call "just in case" covers an entire sheet of paper. Cupboards and fridge burst with food. Not empty like last September. Before walking out the door issue final mandate infused with expectation, "This kitchen will not be a disaster when I return."

Sons glance at each other.

Return. Walk into house at summer's dusk, kitchen is neat. Paul, fine. Ricky too when I see him later. Breathe. We did it. Nothing bad happened to us. We survived. Maybe thrived on this new challenge. Tomorrow regroup for our European adventure. Tonight, look forward to rinsing this day away in a hot shower. Body aching from efforts and emotional energy this quick turnaround took. Little bits of adrenaline asking to be washed out of me. Flowing from skin into drain and away.

Open dishwasher to find a water glass. Find dish after dish full of baked-on but clean, sterilized gunk, staring up me. In overloaded dishwasher. Run once in my forty-eight hour absence. Necessary step of dish rinsing unknown, forgotten, or deemed unnecessary by Ricky and Paul.

Sigh. Small thing, really. Better than previous trips. Kitchen holding greasy frying pans full of last night's dinner or snacks left to soak on the stove. Water swirling between islands of oil. Wadded up napkins, paper towels, and various remains of food wrappings sprinkled throughout kitchen and dining area. Glasses half-filled with water scattered throughout, giving impression that many people live here. But in reality, only two young men reaching for a fresh glass with each new drink. Glasses paired with stray sock or two. Previously worn crumpled on counter or table.

This evening stare back at overloaded, unrinsed, and now chipped dishwasher contents. Dishes doubled in layers not deemed possible by me or manufacturers. Wedged together in geometric masterpiece. How can anyone stuff so many dishes into this tank? I sigh. Begin unloading. Dishes smiling as I rinse, scrub, reload, reflecting my smile. Seeing beyond remains of last night's dinner. Glimpsing glimmers radiating in this beautiful mess. Shining with Ricky and Paul are alive! Creating dirty dishes! Conquering effects and impact of disease, trauma, death, and grief in an earthly resurrection of sorts.

Chipped plates are replaceable. Baked on food is soakable. Dishwasher is fully capable of running again. Joy found inside an everyday appliance, a gift, revealing beautiful, messy, chipped love. Ours to cherish as it grounds us to this life.

Traveling Grief

Eight in the morning. On rooftop. Sun beating through thick air. Sky full of other rooftops, antennas, waving laundry. Dry after an hour of hanging. Wonder where buildings end and land runs free.

Spot nearby park's tree line. Vast estate of old empire now open to the public. Feel better knowing nature's nearness.

Remember other rooftops strewn with antennas. Arable land invisible. Nearby river unseen. Silt's smell mingling with smog. Memory permeated with feeling lost. Like this current moment in residential Rome, Italy.

Our stay here, temporary. Not a grief move or relocation. Crossing ocean or border as emotional refugees. Home no longer existing. Ours, a purposeful fleeing. Intentional escape. On the outside we look relatively as we did before. Some of us taller, some thinner. All with longer hair. Our physical home still standing. Emotional one needing repair. Simpler to flee for a time than reconstruct. Seek sanctuary. Retreat from our truth.

Pulled by intense urges to fly away as soon as the funeral was over. Resist, resist, resist this reaction to run away from our reality. Find focus instead in this trip. Conscious attempt to stem ongoing internal push to avoid pain. Our adventure in tragedy's aftermath poorly planned, paid too much for, and now on. Staying with family. Brother Peter in Germany. Niece Marissa in Rome. Oldest one of our six nieces. The only one Tony called "muffin head."

Now after traveling almost three weeks I hear my inner voice say, "It's time to go home." Except, I'm not sure where home is. Even after so many attempts to convince myself home is in my relationships with Ricky and Paul, Mom, and extended family. But home until last August was in Tony's arms. All other relationships flowing from our home. How can home flow only from me?

Reminders of last time I felt so alone among many. In my twenties living in New York City. Then too, wondering where home was. Thirty years later death's sudden shock throws me into old emotional vortex somehow covered in layers of life's dust. Current life built upon remains of single twenties in New York City. Married years in Chicago, Wisconsin, and Iowa.

Yesterday Marissa took us to a small museum off the tourist path but not far from the Colosseum. In heat of Roman day. Down a road first carved out before the time of Jesus. Into cool layers of place called The Roman Houses, La Casa Romana. First layer of homes beginning around 200 C.E. Fourth and top layer from Middle Ages. Wall's stratums showing place where generations of people birthed, lived, loved, lost, worked, and died. All homes built on what came before them. Even the first layer building on creation.

We wander through the caverns' coolness, sweat drying on our skin, voices echoing off ancient stone walls. My family quiet as we move room to room through narrow passageway discovering wall after wall painted with scenes of ancient life and belief. "Wow," is all I can say.

Realize I am like these houses. Building from within upon my many layers. Construction balanced on past foundations. Home for us recreated on new layer. Slowly.

Leavings

Marissa, Paul, Ricky, and I travel via train to small town of Tivoli, Italy. Spend afternoon hiking down the Parco Villa Gregoriana. Deep ravine full of lush overgrowth, waterfalls, cool air, unearthed artifacts, caves, and gurgling stream. Toward end of hike I stop alone along the stream. The others somewhere else on trail. Watch water talk. Allow its cool breezes to dry my sweaty arms. Know I want to leave behind something in this place of beauty and peace. What from this past year of horror, pain, sorrow, tears, and grief can I throw into this moving water? Leave here? Not carry any longer?

Begin silently naming causes of pain from past two years. Doctors, school officials, teachers, neighbors, the state of Wisconsin. A river. Pastors. Well-meaning others. My list ramps up. Into anger thrown silently into water without raising an arm. Anger at Tony for leaving us. Anger at myself for not understanding what was happening at the beach. Not doing enough to save him. Anger for not being the parent my children needed me to be in the months after his death.

Accumulated buildup falls into the stream. Refuse I will not take home. Whisked away by a small current. Running toward something. Away from me. Large breath escapes. Walk on. Approach last cave on path. Hike almost over.

Know I did something needing doing. Acknowledging death's anger is hard but true. Therapy helps. Faith in a loving and grace-filled God helps. Deciding to drop a heavy bit of baggage into an Italian stream helps. Especially when the wind blows on my back just after, finding my neck, then my face, fanning my heart with a cool breeze. Wind propelling us toward life, not away from it, and in doing so honoring the love Tony carried for people, the unwavering belief he had in God, the knowledge he had in our human ability to heal emotionally no matter the cause or causes of our pain. Most of all, Tony's wish for us to live, to live well by loving others and to love well by loving God. Neither of which we can do traveling burdened by too much luggage.

Dreams

We sit—Ricky, Paul, Marissa, and I—at a long table. In a small restaurant. Down a cobbled, narrow street. In Marissa's Roman neighborhood. On top of one of the seven hills of Rome. Watching trays of steaming pasta pass by. Smells of garlic and basil filling the air. Starving for *pesce* and *polpette*. Hunger dripping with sweat. Staving off growing agitation by reliving day's adventures through ancient ruins, gurgling Roman fountains, and famous paintings.

Clock chiming as we wait. Hearing night's music collection once, twice. Attention caught by an American blues tune. "I have dreams, dreams to remember," the male singer laments.

Silently I think: I too have dreams to remember. Not sleep's dreams. But dreams of what can be or what I want to do. Because dreams sometimes dry up in life. Last fall cleaning out Tony's office, I found a paperweight. One I bought for The Men's Center years ago. On it, a quote by George Elliot. "It's never too late to become what you might have been."

My dreams before Tony included him in many ways. They were not exclusive of him. But dreams with and because of him. Some dreams continue as loving family. Others, like seminary and writing, reconfigure and readjust. Shifting in an act of renegotiation with reality. Some dreams float in air above, invisible, nudging a bit, awaiting recognition.

Our food arrives. We eat, each in our own thoughts. A few days later, we return to Frankfurt, Germany. First morning, I have coffee with my brother as our children sleep. Afterwards, I walk alone to shopping district in his neighborhood. Participate in ancient urban custom of buying daily bread. Begin at our favorite bakery, one of five along this street. Walk into overpowering bread aromas. Stand in line. Order usual. "Zwei Croissants und fünf Croissants mit Schokolade, bitte."

"Mit keinen Nüssen!" the shop's cashier adds reminding me of my daily plea ensuring Paul's safety from dangerous food allergies. Her gesture, tiny. Almost lost in my American style self-absorption.

"Danke," I say.

I load wax-papered bundles into my cloth shopping bag. Wander up the street. Stop at an outdoor fruit stand. Search for bananas. Owners speak to me in English, my foreignness a worn betrayal. Load fruit into bag. Walk up street to a small grocery store. Crowded with daily staples. One aisle devoting itself to wine. Another boasting only coffee. Against the back wall I find bins holding large warm dark pretzels. Buy one, maybe two, for Paul to taste.

Meander home accompanied by rhythm of swinging bag. Memories of a lost dream float above my steps. Dream of living for a time somewhere in Europe where walking out for morning bread and coffee is a habit. Feeding my starved suburban sensorial soul.

Look up, out of day's dreams not knowing where I am. Feel lost on these German city streets. In a maze of what I thought were well-known paths discovered during other visits here. Each time walking these streets multiple times a day for food, supplies, transportation, and lodging. This trip adding to our accumulated days visiting the Bockenheimer Warte neighborhood. Time now equaling a month spread over eight years. "But I have realized my dream," I say to the wind. "Just not as expected."

Today I remember and embrace this dream hatched before Tony, realized with him, and now rediscovered as his memory lives on in my heart. Smells of fresh bread wafting up from gently swinging bag. Smile finding face like new dawn. Tears escaping eyes. Sliding down toward the ground.

Blue Snow

Booked late in my fuzz-brain, balled-up thinking. Economy seats sold out for return flight home. Pay too much money for first class. Still too out of it to care.

Flight out of Frankfurt delayed. Wait in first-class airport lounge. Sample bits from free buffet. Ricky drinks complimentary champagne in fluted glass. I read European magazines. Accept pampering from concierge. Recovering from security check. Patted down by a female official. Watched by armed guard with automatic rifle standing a foot away. My purse full of liquids not encapsulated in quart-sized plastic bags, my bleary thinking neglecting certain realities.

In Reykjavik we rush through customs. Stand in long lines. Follow directions out onto tarmac. Breathe in crisp, clean Icelandic air. Ricky flings his arms wide open allowing as many pores as possible access to clean oxygen. "This air!" he cries.

I follow suit filling up my lungs. Wanting to break away, stay, not board the airplane.

Inside plane Ricky announces, "I am never returning to economy class."

"These seats are like lounger chairs," Paul exclaims.

First class not full. Both sons spread out, taking over a row each. I snuggle under a beautiful quilt, ready for a nap, my drifting off interrupted by offers of magazines, champagne, coffee, dinner menu. Cabin fills with smells of our feast yet to come. Choose veal with traditional Scandinavian Hasselback potatoes. Sons order steak. Moaning quietly as we eat: "This is so good!"

Meal followed by rich Scandinavian coffee. Made with Icelandic water. Stirred with Icelandic cream and two sugar cubes. Using small European coffee spoon. The kind my children ate from when very young. Slowly sip this silk, smiling. Afterwards slip into sleep.

"We are flying over Greenland! We're flying over Greenland!"

Paul shakes me awake. Leads me to his window. Day bright and clear. Snowcapped mountains rise up as if magically attached to the earth. Ice floats in bay of Advent blue water tinged with ocean green. Inlets meet mountains of snow tinged blue sliding into its shores. Snow smooth for miles, interrupted only by wrinkles both straight and crisscrossing. As if a great grandmother held an infant's smooth skin close to her cragged cheek.

Gazing out onto this beauty, I realize something. I want to write once again about something other than our trauma and grief. Maybe our joy. Maybe our lives healed. Maybe my father's Air Force time in Greenland. Maybe I want to cry for one minute instead of one hour or an entire day. Maybe I want to smile more. Maybe I want to feel good most of the time. Maybe I want to live.

Almost Home

I breathe shallow breaths, allowing just enough oxygen in, just enough carbon dioxide out to keep going. Head lies against the headrest in the back seat of car. Trying to sleep. Ricky driving, listening to tunes on his headset. Awake since 2:00 this morning. Fighting return jet lag. Landing in Minneapolis yesterday. Staying the night in a hotel full of people leaving or returning from overseas. Twelve hours after reentry into the country, drove ninety minutes to the scheduled Lyme disease doctor's office south of St. Cloud, Minnesota. Me thinking two months ago that squashing this checkup appointment in today a good idea. Now knowing better.

This morning, I lost my debit card after losing my credit card in Rome. No cash on me. Just Euros. Local banks refuse exchange. Search hotel lobby. Fellow traveler says, "I always carry two credit cards with me in case I lose one." Thanks for your compassion, I think.

Anxiety clutches my heart. Losing this card is too much for me to handle. In jet lag. In grief. In trauma recovery. In single parenting. In life. Anxiety explodes into rants around the hotel room. Waking Paul and Ricky. Paul, sleep still in his eyes, tells me to go to Target. "Just buy prepaid credit cards with your Target card," he says.

"Okay," I reply.

Adrenaline, that evil outcome of trauma, gets me to Target and back.

Ricky's checkup a good one. Healing slower than first predicted, but progressing. Body returning to health despite all that has happened to us. Difference in his overall health from last year gives me much to be thankful for. Teenagers with Lyme disease have an increased suicide rate. Ricky also developed a secondary disease common with Lyme called Mast Cell Activation Syndrome or MCAS, which causes severe and often life-threatening reactions to food. At the height of his illness, Ricky ate only three foods deemed safe—lamb, rice, and pears. My very real fear of losing him in the wake of losing Tony wanes day by day in small gradations, skimming away paper-thin layers of despondency as Lyme's insidiousness backs down.

Pull out of doctor's parking lot facing seven more hours of travel. In back seat tears form behind closed eyelids. Full of fatigue, gratitude, and worry. Worry about fast approaching dates of our wedding anniversary and Tony's death. Remind myself to remember today as first year's anniversary of Ricky's diagnosis with Lyme disease. A moment last year full of life and hope. Then and now, a time of celebration. And maybe we do celebrate in our own way by heading home. Weaving in and out of half-sleep, I think perhaps embracing goodness is something to work on. Remembering Tony saying at dinner after we said grace, "Give me three gratitudes."

Sons groaning in response each time he prompted us to play the gratitude game instead of the complaint game. Looking down at their plates for ideas. Ricky saying, "Steak."

"Mashed potatoes," adding Paul.

"Time with family," my contribution.

Tony finishing. "My beautiful wife. My boys. Our life together."

First Anniversary

Throat parches. Cannot quench my thirst. Head spins. Forcing me to stop preparing dinner. Sit down on sofa. Hunger gnawing away at stomach lining. First time in a year. Then arms ache up and down. As shaking erupts from deep within my body.

Look again at the clock. All day I have been looking at the clock. Retracing the events of one year ago. The rainy morning. The group walk through the farm fields, up the long gravel road to the main road. Tony loving the landscape of prairie fields surrounded by woods. Surveying the fields and forests saying, "I'd love to buy this place."

Drinking in fresh air. Made clean after so much rain. Laughing in delight of it all. Eating lunch together at a long table in the age-old communion of family gathering to feed each other with food, faces, stories, and ideas. Loading up the cars for the beach.

Driving there just the four of us in the quiet of our car. The rest of the family following behind us. A family on vacation. Tony, a little irritated at the boys for not wanting to help unload the kayak. Me, smoothing over the discourse. Aiming toward my goal for all to have a fine day.

Paddle the kayak up the river to our designated beach spot. Fighting a current, the likes never encountered before. Juxtaposed with a beach teaming with human activity. Toddlers digging in the smooth sand of the beach. Some in life vests, some not. Kayak racks everywhere in the parking lot. Noise of humans at play permeating the air.

One year later, I breathe slowly in and out. Waiting. On loveseat. Try standing again. But dizzy, like at the beach. Sit down. Notice clock ticking. Sons elsewhere in the house. Quiet. Not hungry. Cranky. Paul's stomach hurting again. Ricky, anxious. Our bodies replaying the day. The water, waiting on the beach, aftermath. Wait again today. Frozen to furniture. A piece Tony and I picked out early in our marriage. Today hoping, praying that Ricky and Paul stay away from me. I do not want them to witness me relive the day.

5:20 p.m. Must be the time rescue team brought Tony to the ambulance. It must be the time the makeshift curtain separated me from Tony while the paramedics worked on him. Going through the protocol knowing from education and experience Tony no longer lived in any earthly definition. Time of death called twenty minutes later. At 17:40.

Clock keeps ticking. For twenty more minutes. Dizziness passes. Leaving me in an extreme hunger. Realize for the first time how hungry I must have been at the beach. How hungry I have been for an entire year. Remaining hungry, a way of staying in this time of waiting for Tony's return to us. Keeping vigil. Though my body knows more fully one year later he will not be coming back. In future months I will continue looking for Tony when I hear trauma therapist Resmaa Menakem speak at a local bookstore. When I listen to the experts Tony studied with on podcasts during my daily walks. When I continue yearning for his daily embrace. His arms enfolding me, containing my day's pain. Whenever my heart yearns for what was torn away from me, from us.

The next day, the beginning of year two, we return to our lives. Prepare for school and work to begin once again. In therapy, Marit assures me next year will not be as intense. Her words fall on me like gentle snow. Hope infused in its flowery flakes.

Remembrance

Today on this first anniversary of the day we lost so much, we remember Tony.

> His ready smile and easy laugh,
>
> Quirky sense of humor,
>
> Commitment to his work and to his family,
>
> Efforts in building and strengthening his relationships with all of us,
>
> Sacrificial nature,
>
> Humbleness,
>
> Pride and belief in our sons,
>
> Support of me—writing and seminary most of all,
>
> Willingness and big heart,
>
> Love of God, us, and others.

Healing Practice

Dream List: Dreams have a way of slipping away. Getting lost among the list of everyday needs. Write down your past and present dreams. List them in rediscovery and truth.

Prayer

God of our births, lives, deaths, and beyond, thank you for your servants gone before us. Immense clouds soaring in the sky remind us of their witness of you to us then and now. Thank you for those who believe in us, laugh with us, and love us across time and space. Amen.

Stream in Italy from "Leaving."

VII. Wounding Secrets

"Secrets kill. Kill people, yes. Secrets also kill
our relationships and dreams."
—Jennifer Ohman-Rodriguez

"We always have choices. We may not like the choices we have.
But sometimes we have to pick the best one. Even if it's not that
great. But we always have choices."
—Tony Rodriguez

Wounding Secrets

Behind all present or buried emotional trauma live secrets—a
fact clarified to me as a trauma expert's wife. Tony dissected
this stuff in our talks all the time. Partially to let off steam. Partially to bond with me. Partially because my curiosity demanded
it.

All of us were traumatized that day on the beach but could
not figure out the secrets. Not in the beginning. Not now. What
are they? Where are they? Unearthing, a necessary task for
continued healing. Because Tony taught me that secrets perpetuate shame. Shame begets insidious evil. Truth, however, claims
justice and gives life.

Tony's personal and business affairs contained no secrets. A
little more debt on the business than remembered but nothing
out of the ordinary. Most of what I found was predictably Tony—
filing needing to be done, quirky knickknacks, a desk full of work
waiting for his return.

Maybe secrets included a growing brain tumor or approaching heart attack. I wondered many times in those first months if I should have agreed to an autopsy. Science answering mounting questions. Shifting blame from me to a disease. But regardless of a possible autopsy's outcome, a river took Tony's life.

Paul and Ricky held back, not sharing their entire story. Their unspoken experience that day became data I wanted. I pushed for it out of my own need, prompting their retraction. Instead, the story unfolded on their time, supported by therapy, containing no secrets, only a horrendous situation causing normal trauma responses in all of us.

Maybe my overriding sense of guilt held secrets? I revisit the scene in my mind, now more in memory than in flashback. Return to EMDR with Marit, buzzer ticking away. Left hand. Right hand. Echoing off quiet walls. Until something stirs, welling up. Lining throat. Anger screaming. Rolling into betrayal's rage.

Idyllic scene of Peck's Landing, a painted mirage. Beauty and serenity, an opening scene of our true-life horror film. Impending doom lurking beneath landscape's first layer like a monster. A well-known and dangerous undercurrent, unannounced to innocent strangers. Serious realities denied to visitors. Treacherous truths only emerging after Tony slipped away. Never returning alive.

Four people died in the Wisconsin River in August 2016. Two on the same day. About forty miles apart. Tony and a stranger to us. The news coverage tells me three of the four people losing their lives, changing others' lives forever, from out of state. Tourists. Visitors. Strangers. Guests. Parents. Spouses. Children. Human beings.

After this session with Marit, I know I must act. Consider options. Need an opinion, direction. Visit Mom's lawyer instead of my own. Require a woman's advice, a woman's sensibilities. "I grew up on the Mississippi River," I tell her. "A river teaming with boats of all sorts. People sail, ski, tube all summer long.

People swim on island beaches up and down the river. Maybe one person dies a summer. Maybe. But this river, the Wisconsin River, multiple people die in its waters yearly."

Lawyer leans in. "You have an ethical responsibility to sue. There is a traceable history of death here."

Standing next to Tony's grave stone a few days later, tell Ricky of my meeting with lawyer. "A child couldn't survive that current," he says, body intimate with this reality.

Children die in this river. Not one. Many. Almost mine. This lawyer finds me a lawyer in Wisconsin. I tell my mother. She says, "If your father was alive, he would have saved Tony."

My heart plumments. Would my father at age eighty-four still be physically strong enough to prevent this tragedy? Would his thinking capabilities still include his keen sense of safety aware-ness? "Mom, maybe. Maybe not. We don't know if Dad were alive, what condition he would be in now."

Somehow though my actions toward lawsuit give her space to speak the guilt she keeps buried on her heart. Creating some balm. The only time in this journey I provide a small form of comfort to her.

Truth

In a small bistro, Elaine, my widowed pastor and therapist friend, and I talk. Ninety minutes talking around what mixes within me. Until forced to share by Elaine's disclosure about her recent and wonderful trip to Spring Green, Wisconsin. *She doesn't know,* I realize. Breaking in, "It's where Tony died." Words cut air as lungs back into themselves. "In the river near that beach. Next to the Taliesin Visitor's Center."

Elaine quiets. "The beach looks so inviting."

Tears flow in held emotional space. "I keep thinking of what Tony used to say. He'd ask: 'What's the cost of not doing some-thing.' In this case, not suing?"

Tony posed this question so many times in our life together it made me bristle. No decision was ever simple for us. Time taught me to listen to Tony's gut, the bigger picture he saw before me. Left now to listen to my own without his. Feeling not fully trustworthy alone. But all week inner turmoil repeating one message: I am not willing to carry this wounding secret silently. Or even contain it within my family and close friends. We did nothing wrong the day Tony died. Feel forced by unknown others to take blame, a burden that belongs elsewhere. Trauma recovery for all of us requiring continued profound action of me. "I need a lawyer in Wisconsin."

But how to get to Wisconsin? Thought freezes me again. Triggers small PTSD reactions. "I'll drive you." Elaine says.

After lunch in car's security, body erupts into tremors and shakes, making driving sixty miles home impossible, dangerous. Shop instead. Allowing large store to absorb my twitching. Adrenaline's loop racing once more around body's track. Tongue licking lips again and again, aisle by aisle. Something I must have done that day on the beach, in the heat. Dry sun parching my waiting face. Lips wanting to kiss Tony. Our reconciling kiss, a vision haunting me. Lips exchanging fear of what might have happened. Which did happen. Leaving my lips void of Tony's moisture. Instead needing water that day. Repulsed by my own need. Now in this store, nauseated again. Reliant on my shopping list—bagels, lettuce, apples.

Breathing in five counts and out five counts. Aligning my steps with breath. Filling my cart. Remaining dry-eyed in checkout lane. Pushing out into sun through store's massive doors. Sliding into car. Pointing myself toward home. Tears spilling out. Lamenting, "Why God? Why is healing so painful?"

Journal Entry

Around fourteen months.

I want...to attest to this excruciating, exquisite journey. The moments when all is good but pain not over yet. And awful triggered days when time stops once more. Falls back into an abyss, one no longer fitting. Today not hiding in bed as much. Is this progress? Even as guilt revisits me. Adding weight to laden soul. Prohibiting passage into healing. Wondering what I reflect forward? To sons? To world? In healing's mirror? Guilt? Hope? Pray my reflection is freedom. From despair's exile. From grief and trauma's foreign lands. Illuminating possible return. To life fully. Not former life. But life. Carrying inner peace. Radiating joy. As the prophet speaks: "You will go out in joy. Carrying peace."[18]

Discovery

Continue exploring possible litigation. Through a maze of lawyers. Second lawyer, scattered. Pulled between work, aging mother, and daughter. Her inner turmoil recognizable. I too am pulled in every direction possible. This lawyer exhausts me with her exhaustion. "Why did you wait so long?"

"Every widow book and grief expert urges widows to hold off on major decisions for the first year." I retort.

"I have to go," she says. "I'll send you a confirmation email regarding my services."

Something stops me from replying. Second lawyer, a Chicago colleague of first lawyer, calls a few weeks later. Agrees to look into the matter. A week or two go by. Phone rings as I drive.

"Suing will be almost impossible."

Something about a state law against suing for accidents and deaths occurring from recreational activities on either private or public lands. Cites a case in which two young boys die even though there was a lifeguard. Urges me to take the political route by contacting state representatives and writing letters to the editor. Body sinks. Balls up. Protects my heart. Weight of advocating for change plows me under emotionally. "You write," she says. Write I do. But writing for internal solace and under-

---

[18] Isaiah 55:12a (my translation).

standing brings peace. Writing for change requires a far different energy.

My local lawyer pushes me to try one more time. Finds me another lawyer. "Really, nothing can be done," he says. "Maybe you could write letters to elected officials."

"NO! I consider it a personal boundary issue to spend my time, energy, and money to make the necessary changes for saving lives in the state of Wisconsin. This job is the job of its citizenry and elected officials. Not me, the victim of your state's lack of ownership. I have a family to support, trauma to heal, and grief to feel."

Investigating possible litigation uncaps not-so-secret (unless you are a tourist) wounding trauma concealment. Underlying laws creating havoc, inflicting pain, stealing life. Unearthing state's criminality in Tony's death.

Going Back

Ankle deep in cool water. Giving young nieces rides in our kayak. Glancing over again and again to where Tony, Ricky, and Paul are in water downriver. Wondering why they are so far out. Reasoning they are not any farther out than the boys playing near them.

Tony comes in. Don't know where Ricky is. Paul still in the water. "Does Paul know what to do with this current?" I ask.

"I don't know what to do," he says.

And this is where I think I said, "You go with it." But I might have said, "I think you go with it." I'll never know. But these are the last words I spoke to Tony.

All three again in the water. My eyes watching them for what seems like forever. Until they are farther out into the middle of the river than others. Out where boaters putt back and forth ignoring them. Hand kayak rope to my brother. "I need to tell them to come back in."

Walk toward my family. Paul emerges. Walks forward onto beach. Wooden. Stiff. Grey like ash. My body feels some relief. He is safe. Now Ricky walks toward me too. Also stiff. Also grey. My body lets go of something it holds onto. Then Ricky speaks in flat voice void of emotion. Deep in timbre. "Dad's in trouble."

Look toward Tony still in water. Not understanding. Until he disappears. Water filling in space he once occupied.

The beach along Highway 23 between Dodgeville and Spring Green, Wisconsin, always looked inviting. Tony and I visited the area around this same time of year, August. Close to our anniversary. First two times in celebration of five and then ten years of marriage. Always wanting to bring the whole family. To enjoy Shakespeare in the great outdoors. Hike rolling hills. Float down this river in large innertubes. Bring our kayaks to this beach. A beach so flat and large for a river. Not muddy but full of sand.

We brought one kayak on our small family vacation. Two didn't fit with the car top carrier. One was enough. The night before Tony died, all eight of us sitting in a long line, ranging in age from six to eighty-one, enjoying Shakespeare. Tony sitting at one end. I at the other. Bookending our beloveds. Tony tipping his head toward me. Catching my eye. Blinking an "I love you" gesture. His last. To me.

Drove over to beach next afternoon. Calm. Breathing together once again as a family. After being splintered by sons' many illnesses. Once at beach, I paddle upstream, fighting crazy current unusual for so near shore. Mom chooses beach spot. Sits down, book nearby. Others leaving cell phones, shirts, sunglasses. Talking. Like so many times at beaches across Midwest. Full of people, boats, relaxation, and family fun. Ours. Others.

But Tony died this seemingly perfect day. In a river named for or after a state, he died drowning. Dragged below by an unknown and misunderstood undercurrent. Dying because the beach at Peck's Landing was open the day after a heavy rainfall. Full of people swimming, floating, boating, and basking in sun, leading us to believe it was safe, well-tended with safety measures. But not safe at all. River's grasp catching my three beloveds. Ricky and Paul breaking free. Living now with double memories in mind and body. Of their father's demise and their own brush with death.

News reporting never confirmed by me, the sole witness to river yanking Tony under and away. News reports implying he was a non-swimmer. Blaming victim. Taking easy way out. Covering truth.

Tony was an average swimmer. But he was no stranger to natural water, having spent almost every vacation for twenty-two years on the banks of various lakes, rivers, and oceans. He was also careful and safety conscious. Tony would not take ownership for his death. Tony would not allow Ricky and Paul to take ownership for his death. Tony would not allow me to take ownership for his death. Nor shall I take it. Tony's death was preventable in acts of simple citizenry. In small precautions one neighbor does for another. In acts a state does for the common good, the good of all, and not the fun of a few.

Compassion

First responder point person tells me he's also a pastor. A man who lost his father as a child. Tells me, "But the Lord fathered me from then on. He will father your sons as well."

Why am I being subjected to this type of Christianity? When I am standing on a beach waiting for the first responder diving team to find Tony? Standing here alone, with no protection. No advocate for my well-being. Walling me off from dangerous, shallow platitudes? Mom pines for Dad to be here to avoid this tragedy. I want him here to protect me from this man's preying god. And also the older, heavyset man with voice betraying his allergies. The one saying to me "There's really no hope, you know."

The man I demand the first responder pastor person dismiss. Because I've now had enough additional emotional abuse at the beach. My voice somehow finding itself through shut-down brain. Erupting with words. Delivered in strength. "Get rid of him or I will implode!"

Vulnerability became my voice on the day I met trauma and grief. And while it has taken months for me to say that vulnerability no longer poses certain risk factors to my well-being and that of my sons, I still claim it as the beginnings of a new kind of inner courage. A courage born out of a moment when all unnecessary layers of life vanished. Washed away. Beneath dangerously unmarked treacherous river. As I watched. Shaking within. Falling into fragility keeping me company for months.

I say there is an incredible strength in grief and beauty worn in mourning and unasked for wisdom found in trauma recovery. The kind of strength called courage. Mourning which can only be called love. And wisdom needed to speak into the wrongs of this world. To apply weakness to this time, experience, body sensations, and feelings is to shame the throbbing tenderness of life itself.

Another first responder, someone who tried so very hard to bring life back into Tony's beautiful body, said goodbye to me with tears in his eyes on the day that everything changed. And then he hugged me with a fierceness I will never forget. Showing me living courage. Giving me his vulnerability and compassion. Sharing a moment of unmasked emotion as I recognized in him what became my truth.

Board Ship Here

Next to Tony's computer at The Men's Center sat a photo of us, taken by my mother or father, I don't remember which. We stand on the dock at Ludington, Michigan, windblown, tanned, young, in love. Waiting for the Lake Michigan ferry to take us across to Wisconsin. To our car pointing us toward home. Our heads touching lightly in front of a sign. Words reading,

BOARD
SHIP
HERE

And we did. We boarded a ship toward home. The one we made with each other. Boarded a ship called love, marriage, parenthood, followers of dreams and vocation. Now called devastation, loss, grief, trauma, but still called home and always called love.

Some years our ship sailed smoothly. Some years we endured turbulence. But ultimately all our years perpetuated love, commitment, and a willingness to show up each day. Ours was not a perfect trip, not even close. But it was ours in our own "for better and for worse."

What occurs next on this ship without my cocaptain remains to be seen. The good news is there is an after, a next, a future for us. Sustainable health for Ricky and Paul and continued good health for me. Education for each of us. Maybe a move across town or country. Or then again maybe embracing the house we have. The one Tony deemed "a good house" in the months before he died.

The need for future justice in Tony's death and the many other lives lost in the Wisconsin River pushes me forward into what I do not know. But this something which includes an apology, a simple apology, lives close to my heart.

Whatever future holds, it lives in an ongoing continual unfolding of love between the three of us. Stirred in with sprinkled memories. Along with a phrase said like a broken record under Tony's breath. "That's goodness."

There's a thought: future as goodness. Words by which I live having loved Tony, having learned from him. Still hearing him in the thump, thump, thump of my heart. Stay on the ship, my heart says. Your compass guiding you home to smiles of two young men with their father's eyebrows. A bit of his sense of humor. Delivered in voices an octave lower. Home to dreams of writing and ordination. Home to dentist appointments, errands, family dinner nights, and eating yet another burger joint meal. Home to bills, perpetual home maintenance, a yard once again in need of mowing, or a driveway full of fresh snow. Home to head colds and laundry and a much-needed supportive text from a friend. Home to ongoing monetary uncertainty, trauma recovery, schooling, and aging beloveds. Home to uncomfortable but necessary conversations with our sons about all they face in trauma and grief juxtaposed with their generation's culture.

T.S. Eliot once wrote, "Home is where one starts from."[19]

Words framed, to the left of our well-traveled back door. Reminding me I am home. Home knowing Tony and I created this relational space together and over time. Home wrapping us in love. Home knowing our home didn't drown that day.

Rewrite.

"In the absence of data, the mind makes up stuff."— Tony[20]

Ricky swims against the current at first in a burst of adrenaline. Then not knowing if he has the strength to continue. Paul keeps hand on Tony's upper arm. Tony's eyes close. Head tilts back. All three caught as undertow forces them farther into the river. River moving them toward overpass. Boys running along the shore shouting to them. "Swim sideways!"

Paul follows directions. Ricky uses his strength to change direction. Both walk out of water. To life. Tony knowing even in

---

[19] "The Four Quartets: V," The Poetry Archive, accessed February 17, 2021, https://poetryarchive.org/poem/four-quartets-extract/.

[20] Based on quote by Brené Brown "In the absence of data, we will always make up stories." Found in her book *Rising Strong: How the Ability to Reset Transforms the Way We Live, Love, Parent, and Lead* (New York: Random House, 2015), 79.

body ravaged with shock that his sons are safe. River then taking him under. Away. As I watch amid current's deadly swirls. My body in full alarm for both him and myself.

Once inside the river, Tony reaches out. For help. A hand reaches in, grasping him. Not from land or boat. From beyond. A voice from the past. One full of love saying, "I've got you Tony Boy. Sleep."

And you do, my love. Fall into a restful, peaceful sleep. More healing than all the scarce minutes you slept the past year. A sleep of bliss. You wake, surrounded by those who love you. On earth and in heaven. Some holding you with tears. Some with joy. Depending on what plane your loves reside. Within this circle, you and I hold each other in love. Sprinkled with forgiveness for what we could not control.

In the absence of data, my mind makes up parts of this story. Creates missing pieces. Strung together with scavenged leftovers from the day. Pieced together with love. Into story. Sons making it to safety. The rest, the best imagined scenario under horrific circumstances.

Coda

A deep, resonant bell rings over the water at Peck's Landing near Spring Green, Wisconsin, rippling the water with its hollow yet haunting sound, disrupting dawn with pain and longing. Its tones forming red rose petals. Its vibrations mixing with air mixing with mist mixing with sorrow mixing with love. Petals fall into currents escaping bell's truth. Only earth witnessing quiet tears of ages. Bell striking. Pealing out. Naming each life lost in this treacherous river. Tolling on and on and on. Seeming as if it cannot stop. So many torn from life. Sacrificed in river's rapid, clutching arms. River waiting hungrily for more. Bell tolling. Adding each life left to mourn.

We stand, strangers, on river's banks. Listening to our heart's pain. Waving. Blowing kisses. Shouting "Goodbye!" and "We love you!" and "Still!" We stand doing all we could not do that day. Allowing our bodies, our containers of emotions, to move in ritualized acts of closure. Finally.

I stand watching the river's current flow quickly under the bypass bridge. Right arm raised in wave. Sinking slowly to shoulder level. Fingers curling. Hand clutching hand no longer in mine. Tears dropping on shirt. Eyes unwilling to leave scene of last seeing. Pain rolling up out of my body's center. Creating waves in stomach, chest, jaw, and breath. Hands slowly covering my mouth in horror, disbelief, panic, and truth.

I breathe. Drop hand to side. Watch last of rose petals disappear. As light wanes toward night. Leaving me alone. Standing statue. Memorializing Tony's essence. Offering only words making meaning in my betrayed, bereaved heavy heart.

Still my love. Still.

Healing Practice

Imagining: Today in your journal envision and imagine healing choices for yourself and your beloveds. Begin with the choices you do have. Add methods you've read about or heard about which interest you. Even if there are no practitioners near you or any money to pay for these services. Write everything down as dreams, hopes, and prayers. Read your list. Every day.

Truth that Needs Saying

Healing from trauma is a basic human right. Yet it continues to be limited or denied to people in our country because of historic ingrained and perpetuated racism, biases, and powering over systems. Who heals from traumatic experiences depends on availability of health insurance, money, time, affordability, and access. Those of us who heal have healing methods available to us for unjust reasons while others continue to suffer.

Prayer

God of embrace and release, of cleaving and letting go, bring us into continued life. Rebuild homes. Restore dreams. Reignite passions. Relieve trauma's pain for every person in need. Remove healing barriers. Dismantle systems that perpetuate trauma. Lessen financial burdens. Make available more options and choices. Encourage hearts and minds to bear long-kept secrets safely into the hands of true healers. Amen.

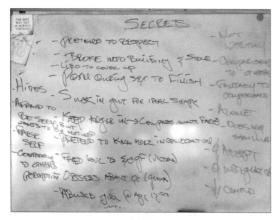

White board from group session at The Men's Center focusing on secrets.

Boarding the Ludington, Michigan ferry, 1996.

Photo of Tony with his parents and sister Riphanie.

About to cross the headwaters of the Mississippi River in 2011.

Gratitude

No project this deeply personal ventures into literary life without a crew of others. My gratitude abounds for Rev. Linda K. Lund, Rev. Peter W. Marty, Cynthia Weeks, and Scott Teasdale, love in the worst hours of our lives. For family in all our collective ups and downs: Mom and Dad. Peter, Jamie, Marissa, Christina, Angela, Cassandra, Matilda, Grace, Joe, and Mick. Especially Riphanie, for all you do for all of us. For Tony's parents, Rick and Hope, for raising such a beautiful son. For beloved sons Ricardo and Paul for saying "okay" to this work. For Solstead Women, Erin Anderson, Rev. Dr. Jan Schnell, Rev. Sarah Goettsch. ELCA congregations, St. Paul (Davenport), Gloria Dei, and JustChurch (Iowa City), and St. Andrew (Cedar Rapids). For the Southeastern Iowa Synod of the ELCA, Bishops Michael Burk and Amy Current. Rev. Paul Ostrem. Rev. Elaine Olson, Dawn Rundman, Ethel Barker, Deb Hetherington, Luther Seminary faculty and staff, Cohort Ten, Steve Semken, Misty Urban, Wendy Henrichs, Katherine House, Sister Ann Jackson, Lori Erickson, Kate Sheehan Roach, Brian Allain, and Brad Lyons, Deborah Arca, Indu Guzman and the rest of the crew at Chalice Press. For healing professionals showing therapy in its many forms as embodiments of love and sacrifice: Marie Garry, LMHC; Meg Eginton, MFA, RSME-T; Kate Gleeson, MA, LISW; Phil Striegel, MFT, Ph.D.; and Randall R. Lyle, MFT, Ph.D.

Tony closed his gratitude page in *Facing Heartbreak* with these words:

"Lastly, to my amazing and beautiful wife, Jennifer, I adore you. Without your fearless words of confidence and support I would have not been able to pursue my dreams and complete this book. It is with you that I share my completeness and humanity. You are my bliss and my love (still and always)."[21]

Tony, there would be no book without you. Not because you died. But because you loved me. Because you encouraged my creative space for years. Because of the lasting gifts you left me, fully realized without you here. As you used to say, "You are in my heart." Still and always, my love.

Tony's professional photo taken in his office.

---

[21] Stefanie Carnes, Mari A. Lee, and Anthony D. Rodriguez, *Facing Heartbreak: Steps to Recovery for Partners of Sex Addicts* (Carefree, AZ: Gentle Path Press, 2012), ix.

Tony's Sayings

Hope lives in the work of healing.

Everyone is annoying sometimes.

What would the observer say?

Do you want to feel better or do better?

What about the gal at ground zero?

Make new data.

Are you guessing?

Give me three gratitudes.

Let the scream out.

This is about the little girl.

Find a safe place or room.

How does that resonate with you?

Give me a high and a low.

Do you want to be seen or do you want to be noticed?

That's goodness.

You're working off old data.

Executive logic.

Find the baby.

Are you safe enough?

Stay in the space.

Two feelings words (Give me two feeling words.)

Activated.

What just happened here?

Don't forget your tool box.

The guy at ground zero goes to the bunker.

How's that working for you?

So this is all about you?

Low-hanging fruit.

Write a new narrative.

This is about the little boy.

Get in the pit.

That's your humanity.

That sounds like whoo whoo to me.[22]

You always have choices.

You are always in my heart.

Sayings Tony said to clients during therapy sessions.

---

[22] Attributed to Phil Striegel, MFT, Ph.D.

Helping

People often ask me how to best serve others in trauma's aftermath and recovery. They want a "to do" list followed by a "what not to do list." Because most people want to do the right thing for those they love and support. At best, however, a checklist alleviates the helper's anxiety about using correct supportive behavior. In other words, the checklist, as Tony would put it, is all about them, the giver of care and support and not the person suffering.

Right now, some of you are resisting that the checklist is about your stuff. OK. Sit with this thought. Where does your resistance reside in your body? (Some of you are saying "Ouch!" right now).

Here's another list that is also about you, the person who wants to help and support. But not in the way the security blanket checklist is. This list is about your pain and how your unhealed pain affects other people. So if you really want to do well in helping others suffering from trauma's afterlife, here are the basics:

1. Admit you, the one who wants to help, may—probably— have unhealed trauma living in your body. So if you really still want to help, the best action you can take is to begin your own healing journey in trauma recovery.

2. If you are well into your own healing process, climb down into the pit of suffering and despair with the person you want to help and support. Yes, climb down into their ashes. Sit there with them in quiet. And if you hear yourself talking, STOP! Please stop prattling on and on about nothing because you are nervous about being a pit dweller with your person.

3. While you are being quiet, remind yourself to bury your platitudes. Throw them away. They are garbage, refuse cluttering up your life and the lives of others.

4. Staying quiet gives you time to breathe slowly in and even more slowly out. Your breath creates peace within you, the kind of peace you give without words to your suffering person.

5. When your breath has settled you, begin listening by observing your person. Use observation as a form of prayer.

6. Sometimes speaking is necessary when sitting with suffering ones. We can share balm and alleviate a layer of pain by learning simple techniques for what is called emotional trauma first aid. These techniques when used take some of the stress off of a person's agitated nervous system. Anyone can learn these techniques and apply them. Here are two places to begin:

    a. The SCOPE Safety Aid at https://traumahealing.org/scope/

    b. EmotionAid® video from The International Trauma Healing Institute at https://www.youtube.com/watch?v=Ab-jeuwWnmc

*The day in 2012 we found Tony's book on the shelves at
Prairie Lights Bookstore in Iowa City, Iowa.*

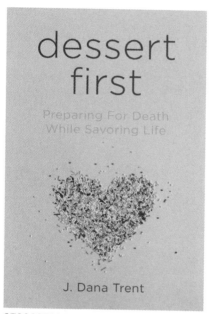

9780827206694, $16.99

Foreword Indies Book of the Year Award, Bronze Winner, Grief/Grieving

"Dessert First is an exceptionally well-written, in-
spired, and inspiring book. Trent's perspective would
appeal to readers across most faith traditions, and
even many who wouldn't be inclined to pick up a
work like this."— *Shelf Awareness*

chalice press
You Want to Change the World. So Do We.

Order at chalicepress.com
or where books are sold

9780827233140, $16.99

"How do you talk to a child about death? Start here. This beautiful book helps contextualize loss, and provides a beautiful memory to share with the family member who will be left behind."
—Jodi Picoult, #1 NYT bestselling author of *The Book of Two Ways*

chalice press
You Want to Change the World. So Do We.

Order at chalicepress.com or where books are sold